Speak UP, Speak OUT!

THE EXTRAORDINARY LIFE OF "FIGHTING SHIRLEY CHISHOLM"

Speak UP, Speak OUT!

THE EXTRAORDINARY LIFE OF "FIGHTING SHIRLEY CHISHOLM"

By Coretta Scott King Honor Winner
Tonya Bolden

With a foreword by
Stacey Abrams

NATIONAL GEOGRAPHIC

Washington, D.C.

Published by National Geographic Partners, LLC

Since 1888, the National Geographic Society has
funded more than 14,000 research, conservation,
education, and storytelling projects around the
world. National Geographic Partners distributes
a portion of the funds it receives from your
purchase to National Geographic Society to
support programs including the conservation
of animals and their habitats. To learn more,
visit natgeo.com/info.

For more information, visit
nationalgeographic.com, call 1-877-873-6846,
or write to the following address:

National Geographic Partners
1145 17th Street N.W.
Washington, DC 20036-4688 U.S.A.

For librarians and teachers:
nationalgeographic.com/books/librarians-
and-educators

More for kids from National Geographic:
natgeokids.com

National Geographic Kids magazine inspires
children to explore their world with fun yet
educational articles on animals, science, nature,
and more. Using fresh storytelling and amazing
photography, *Nat Geo Kids* shows kids ages 6
to 14 the fascinating truth about the world—
and why they should care. **natgeo.com/subscribe**

For rights or permissions inquiries, please contact
National Geographic Books Subsidiary Rights:
bookrights@natgeo.com

Designed by Julide Dengel

Library of Congress Cataloging-in-
Publication Data

Names: Bolden, Tonya, author.
Title: Speak up, speak out! : the extraordinary life
    of "fighting Shirley Chisholm" / by Tonya
    Bolden.
Other titles: Extraordinary life of "fighting Shirley
    Chisholm"
Description: Washington, DC : National
    Geographic, 2022. | Includes bibliographical
    references and index. | Audience: Ages 8-14 |
    Audience: Grades 4-6
Identifiers: LCCN 2021011555 (print) | LCCN
    2021011556 (ebook) | ISBN 9781426372360
    (hardcover) | ISBN 9781426372377 (library
    binding) | ISBN 9781426372957 (ebook)
Subjects: LCSH: Chisholm, Shirley,
    1924-2005--Juvenile literature. | African
    American legislators--Biography--Juvenile
    literature. | Women legislators--United
    States--Biography--Juvenile literature. |
    Legislators--United States--Biography--
    Juvenile literature. | United States. Congress.
    House--Biography--Juvenile literature. |
    African American presidential candidates--
    Biography--Juvenile literature. | Women
    presidential candidates--United States--
    Biography--Juvenile literature. | Presidential
    candidates--United States--Biography--
    Juvenile literature. | Brooklyn (New York,
    N.Y.)--Biography--Juvenile literature. | New
    York (N.Y.)--Biography--Juvenile literature.
Classification: LCC E840.8.C48 B65 2022 (print) |
    LCC E840.8.C48 (ebook) | DDC 328.73/092
    [B]--dc23
LC record available at https://lccn.loc
    .gov/2021011555
LC ebook record available at https://lccn.loc
    .gov/2021011556

Printed in the United States of America
21/WOR-PCML/1

For Brooklyn!

In the pages of this book, you will explore the life of Shirley Chisholm with the help of newspaper articles and books from the time period. All quoted material appears exactly as it appeared in the source. We have capitalized "Black" when it is used outside of direct quotes and refers to a person or group of people, to reflect the shared identity of the Black community.

★ ★ ★ ★ ★ ★ ★ ★ ★ ★

CONTENTS

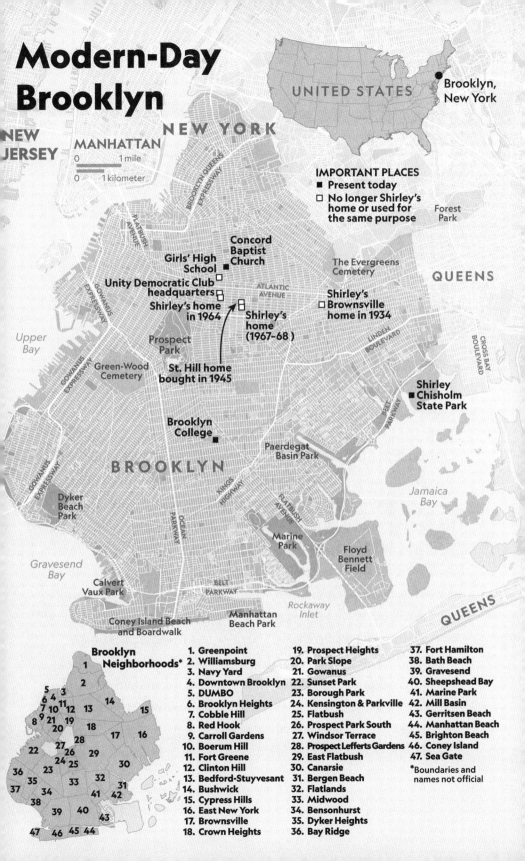

Modern-Day Brooklyn

UNITED STATES

Brooklyn, New York

NEW JERSEY

NEW YORK

MANHATTAN

0 — 1 mile
0 — 1 kilometer

IMPORTANT PLACES
■ Present today
□ No longer Shirley's home or used for the same purpose

Forest Park

QUEENS

BROOKLYN QUEENS EXPRESSWAY

FLATBUSH AVENUE

Girls' High School

Concord Baptist Church

The Evergreens Cemetery

Unity Democratic Club headquarters

ATLANTIC AVENUE

Shirley's home in 1964

Shirley's home (1967–68)

Shirley's Brownsville home in 1934

GOWANUS EXPRESSWAY

Upper Bay

Prospect Park

LINDEN BOULEVARD

CROSS BAY BOULEVARD

Green-Wood Cemetery

St. Hill home bought in 1945

Shirley Chisholm State Park

BELT PARKWAY

Brooklyn College

BROOKLYN

Paerdegat Basin Park

Jamaica Bay

KINGS HIGHWAY

Dyker Beach Park

OCEAN PARKWAY

FLATBUSH AVENUE

Marine Park

Floyd Bennett Field

Gravesend Bay

Calvert Vaux Park

BELT PARKWAY

Coney Island Beach and Boardwalk

Manhattan Beach Park

Rockaway Inlet

QUEENS

Brooklyn Neighborhoods*

1. Greenpoint
2. Williamsburg
3. Navy Yard
4. Downtown Brooklyn
5. DUMBO
6. Brooklyn Heights
7. Cobble Hill
8. Red Hook
9. Carroll Gardens
10. Boerum Hill
11. Fort Greene
12. Clinton Hill
13. Bedford-Stuyvesant
14. Bushwick
15. Cypress Hills
16. East New York
17. Brownsville
18. Crown Heights
19. Prospect Heights
20. Park Slope
21. Gowanus
22. Sunset Park
23. Borough Park
24. Kensington & Parkville
25. Flatbush
26. Prospect Park South
27. Windsor Terrace
28. Prospect Lefferts Gardens
29. East Flatbush
30. Canarsie
31. Bergen Beach
32. Flatlands
33. Midwood
34. Bensonhurst
35. Dyker Heights
36. Bay Ridge
37. Fort Hamilton
38. Bath Beach
39. Gravesend
40. Sheepshead Bay
41. Marine Park
42. Mill Basin
43. Gerritsen Beach
44. Manhattan Beach
45. Brighton Beach
46. Coney Island
47. Sea Gate

*Boundaries and names not official

FOREWORD

BY STACEY ABRAMS, POLITICIAN, LAWYER,
AND VOTING RIGHTS ACTIVIST

★ ★ ★ ★ ★ ★ ★ ★ ★

HISTORY HAPPENS EVERY DAY. IF WE'RE LUCKY, HOWEVER, WE CAN TRACE THE MOMENT OF ORIGIN, TRAVEL ALONG THE PATHWAYS OF DECISIONS MADE AND DISCOVER HOW THE WORLD AND REAL LIVES CHANGED. FOR ME, THAT IS SHIRLEY CHISHOLM'S STORY.

I grew up in southern Mississippi, the daughter of a librarian and a shipyard worker. My parents cultivated a life for me and my five siblings that urged us to imagine opportunities beyond the limits of our environment. My mom and dad grew up during segregation in the Deep South, being told that because of their Blackness, they were inferior to their white peers. For my mother, being a girl was another challenge. Mom and Dad told us about the hardships of poverty and the meanness of laws that sent them to broken schools. They also told us about their time in the civil rights movement, when they marched and picketed and helped others register to vote. Even though they were young and still in school, my parents and their friends were social justice warriors. My parents made certain we knew the tales of civil rights leaders and the lesser-known foot soldiers—those who fought oppression but rarely received any recognition.

As much as my parents ensured we understood the terrible history of segregation, they also taught us to be present in our pursuit of justice. We volunteered in soup kitchens, homeless shelters, and juvenile detention centers. My parents took us with them to vote for every election. We discussed politics in our family as a way to learn about our responsibilities as citizens. Yet, until I was in high school, I had never heard of Shirley Chisholm. (In my parents' defense, I may not have been paying attention.)

My first real encounter with the gutsy gentlelady from New York came when I watched a program about the 1972 presidential election. The retrospective detailed the chaotic race for the White House. Most of the attention focused on the two Georges: George McGovern, the eventual Democratic nominee, and George Wallace, the avowed white supremacist. Congresswoman Chisholm's historic candidacy received very little attention by comparison. In my high school, teachers made no mention of her being the first Black woman from a major political party to run for president of the United States.

How we imagine ourselves in the world often depends on what we know of our past. I could recount those who'd sought to divide our nation during the Civil War and the newly freed Black men elected to Congress during Reconstruction. But I had not learned that Shirley Chisholm was America's first Black woman in Congress. Our nation's history as I knew it was incomplete. And so was I.

Representative Shirley Chisholm did not become president of the United States. She didn't have to do so to change the world. By daring to run—first for Congress and then for the presidency—she gifted us a story about possibility, about resilience, and about destiny. Her story became woven in the history of our nation, and her legacy has spurred the dreams of those who tried what had not been done before.

If Harriet Tubman, stout-hearted, aggressive conductor of the pre Civil War Underground Railroad, could be reincarnated, her spirit would undoubtedly find comfortable lodgings in Shirley St. Hill Chisholm ...

Every identity of the former finds fresh reflection in the latter—short stature, dark skin, sparkling eyes, raw courage, combativeness, and a fierce tenacity for overcoming obstacles.

—New York lawmaker and author
George R. Metcalf, 1971

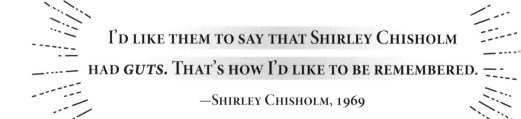

I'd like them to say that Shirley Chisholm had *guts*. That's how I'd like to be remembered.

—Shirley Chisholm, 1969

PROLOGUE

TUESDAY, JANUARY 25, 1972.

She didn't opt for some grand, glittering hotel ballroom or other fancy-schmancy place.

Instead, she chose the auditorium of an elementary school in Bedford-Stuyvesant, a Brooklyn neighborhood better known as Bed-Stuy.

Bed-Stuy had been her home for more than 30 years when she made her historic announcement in that auditorium.

"I stand before you today as a candidate for the Democratic nomination for the presidency of the United States of America."

After a skinny beat—tremendous applause.

"I am not the candidate of black America, although I am black and proud."

Another pile-on of applause.

"I am not the candidate of the women's movement of this country, although I am a woman and I'm equally proud of that."

Before a crowd of about 500 people, so many of them Black women, this lithe, lively woman with a discernible lisp also stated that she was definitely not the candidate of bigwigs and fat cats—oh, no!

Shirley Chisholm was the candidate of and for "the *people* of America," the workaday folk who make up most of the nation.

This gutsy, plainspoken, outspoken woman declared that her presence before the crowd symbolized "a new era in American political history."

And she was on fire for a new America.

An America free of poverty.

An America liberated from all kinds of discrimination.

An America with good jobs, good housing, good health care for everybody.

I stand before you today as a candidate for the Democratic nomination for the presidency of the United States of America.

Never before had a Black woman sought to be the presidential nominee of a major U.S. political party.

Washington, D.C.'s *Sunday Star* called this electric Bed-Stuy moment "a breath-taking expedition to the very Everest of self-confidence."

Self-confidence could have been Shirley Chisholm's middle name.

Along with resolute.

Defiant too.

Self-confident, resolute, and defiant is just what she had needed to be to become Brooklyn's first Black woman elected to the New York State Assembly in 1964.

Self-confident, resolute, and defiant is just what she had needed to be to become America's first Black woman elected to the U.S. Congress in 1968.

And, yes, on this cold 1972 day with Old Man Winter about to sock New Yorkers with an even colder night, Shirley Chisholm had the self-confidence to officially throw her hat into the ring for the highest office in the land.

In doing so, Shirley Chisholm was calling on women and men, people of all ages, of all races and ethnicities to join her in her campaign to move America closer to being its best self.

★ ★ ★

America had a long way to go when it came to that, but Shirley Chisholm and a whole lot of other folks had hope. The nation had already come quite a long way since she was born Shirley Anita St. Hill 47 years earlier on a partly cloudy New York City Sunday, when no one could have predicted that she would one day be such a catalyst for change.

★ ★ ★ ★ ★ ★ ★ ★ ★ ★

CHAPTER 1

USE IT

"YOU MUST MAKE SOMETHING OF YOURSELVES."

"God gave you a brain; use it."

That was Charles Christopher St. Hill firmly but lovingly fueling his "Shirls" and her younger sisters with the can-do, must-do spirit.

Looking to make something of *himself*, years earlier, in April 1923, Charles boarded the S.S. *Munamar*, a 3,477–gross ton passenger-cargo ship that would take him from Antilla, Cuba, to the United States. The ship's passenger list had him down as a 22-year-old shoemaker.

A few days later, the Statue of Liberty was in view. Soon Charles and other passengers were ferried to Ellis Island, New York Harbor's military fort turned national gateway.

On Ellis Island, Charles joined a cram of humanity. His British-based creole mingled maybe with Sicilian, Lithuanian, Latvian, Russian. Likely Yiddish too.

Whatever their mother tongue, with their luggage in hand, these people trudged into the Main Building via the Baggage Room, then climbed a long flight of stairs to the noisy, cavernous Registry Room on the second floor, later nicknamed the Great Hall.

Anyone spotted out of breath—or in any kind of distress—was pulled aside and checked out. Heart disease? Lung problem?

Those not pulled aside were not necessarily in the clear. Another doctor eyed them like a hawk, on the lookout for such things as strange posture or gait.

Eventually everyone underwent a medical inspection.

Faces were checked for signs of "defects."

Vision tests were administered.

Stethoscopes were pressed to chests to check hearts and lungs.

Nails, skin, and scalps were inspected for infectious diseases.

The medical inspection was just one part of this coming-to-America process that could last for three or more hours—and result in some folks being booted out of the country for medical or other reasons.

Having survived the Ellis Island ordeal, Charles headed to the western tip of another island—Long Island.

★ ★ ★

New York City's bustling borough of Brooklyn, located on Long Island, had about two million residents when Charles arrived. The majority of them were Irish, Italian, Polish, and white people of other ethnicities. Black Brooklynites were less than 2 percent of the population, roughly 32,000 souls. Some African. Some African American. Some West Indian like Charles, a tall, slender man whose hair went white in his early 20s.

According to a grown-up Shirls, Charles was born in British Guiana (now the independent nation Guyana) and lived for years in another British colony, Barbados, before moving to Cuba, likely for work on a sugarcane plantation. But, in a document from the 1940s, Charles affirmed that he was born in Christ Church, Barbados.

In any event, we know for sure that Charles regarded himself first and foremost as Barbadian, or Bajan. Not surprisingly, after he arrived in the United States he fell in with Brooklyn's tight-knit Bajan community with its cricket matches, its socials, and a young seamstress named Ruby Seale, someone he'd known in Barbados.

About a year before Charles sailed to the States, Ruby, on the cusp of 21, left Christ Church, Barbados, aboard the S.S. *Pocone*, a 6,750–gross ton steamer. It brought her to New York City on March 8, 1922.

Ruby and Charles's acquaintanceship in Barbados eddied into courtship in Brooklyn. Then came marriage, and on November 30, 1924, Shirley Anita St. Hill was born.

In spring 1926 she got a little sister, Odessa. In winter 1928 she got another one, Muriel.

The St. Hill family, it seems, was a happy one, with Mummy and Papa doing the very best that they could for their girls.

★ ★ ★

You must make something of yourselves.
God gave you a brain; use it.

Sadly, Shirls' parents weren't able to make much of themselves. Economically, that is. Charles, with a fifth-grade education, was a helper at a Brooklyn bakery. Ruby, with a sixth-grade education, took in sewing jobs.

Poor in pocket, Ruby and Charles were rich in ambition. They longed to own one of Brooklyn's beautiful Victorian brownstone homes. They were also keen to see their daughters go to college. This was at a time when many Americans didn't even have a high school diploma.

To realize their dreams, Shirls' parents knew that they had to work, work, *work.*

But they had limited job opportunities. So did most Black people in Brooklyn, and most Black people in the North. While "Whites Only" and "Colored Only" signs weren't as common as they were in the South, segregation (also known as Jim Crow) and overall anti-Black feelings were very much alive.

Being Black in Brooklyn generally meant being relegated to the lowest-paying jobs because most white-owned businesses wouldn't hire Black people as managers and in other higher-paying jobs. And while there were Black-owned businesses in New York City, there weren't *that* many.

In the 1920s, if Shirls' mom scanned help-wanted ads in, say, the *Brooklyn Daily Eagle,* the jobs she had a shot at had ads that began like this: "GIRL, colored; part time; for housework."

At the time, roughly 70 percent of Black women in New York City were domestic workers, from cooks and cleaners to maids and nannies—jobs that didn't pay a lot.

The low-paying jobs many Black men in Brooklyn were holding down included that of messenger, janitor, dockworker at the Brooklyn Navy Yard, and baker's helper.

True, a lot of white men, especially immigrants, were also in low-paying jobs—moving-van helpers, peddlers of foodstuffs, cooks on tugboats, bricklayers. But a Giuseppe Macaluso from Italy or a Lazer Obstack from Austria had the advantage of white skin—or near-white skin. To be sure, there was prejudice against foreign-born whites, but Black people were still generally the last hired in boom times and the first fired when the economy tanked.

★ ★ ★

Work. Work. *Work.*

To give work their all, Shirls' parents made a tough decision, one that likely at times brought tears to their eyes.

★ ★ ★ ★ ★ ★ ★ ★ ★

CHAPTER 2

WITH COURAGE

RUBY AND CHARLES'S DECISION WAS TO HAVE THEIR
daughters live in Christ Church, Barbados, with Ruby's mom, Emily
Seale, an aunt, and an uncle.

A grown-up Shirls wrote that her mom took her and her sisters to
Barbados "early in 1928" aboard "an old steamer named the *Vulcania.*"

But this doesn't quite match with records. For example, the *Vulcania*
wasn't an old steamer. It was a motor ship, an Italian luxury liner that
wasn't even oceangoing in early 1928. It's more likely that Ruby took the
girls to Barbados in late 1928.

Given that Shirls was a little kid at the time, when she later wrote
of the journey she probably relied on family lore, often a smorgasbord of
mix-ups, of memories playing tricks.

Whatever the ship's name, whenever its departure, about a week later
it docked in Bridgetown, the capital of an island whose shape is likened to
a pear or a leg of mutton. An island a mere 20 miles long and 15 miles
wide and some 40 years away from gaining its independence from
Great Britain.

———— ★ ★ ★ ————

Granny Seale lived in the village of Vauxhall, in a home Shirls remembered as a big frame house with lots of rooms. From the parlor with its
"straight-backed bamboo chairs" to the kitchen with its "old-fashioned
coal range and innumerable cast-iron kettles, pots, and frying pans,"

that home was "elaborately furnished with the two necessities: warmth and love."

But the village of Vauxhall was creepy at first. "The night noises bothered us city children for a long time: the clucking of chickens hit by cars when they dawdled in the road, the cows mooing and sheep bleating, the crickets, and all the unidentifiable sounds around a farm after dark."

Granny was also a bit scary at first. So strict-strict. But Shirls and her sisters soon learned that the woman had nothing but wonderful intentions: To instill in them the can-do spirit. Time and again Granny told Shirls, "Child, you've got to face things with courage."

School was one of those things.

★ ★ ★

Barbados was famous for how seriously it took its British-based schooling. Strict. Strict. *Strict.*

"When you started school here in Barbados, you went right into reading and writing and arithmetic," recalled Shirls' sister Muriel. "There was no such thing as kindergarten and playing around with paper." Kids were in school to *work!*

Learning to read, write, and do arithmetic.

Learning British history.

Perfecting penmanship.

Shirls did that and more in a white wooden one-room school where the day began at eight o'clock in the morning and ended at four o'clock in the afternoon.

Work, work, *work!*

And there was work to do on Granny's farm.

Feeding those clucking chickens (that didn't get hit by cars).

Milking those mooing cows.

Minding those bleating sheep.

There were ducks, goats, and pigs too.

Plus, buckets of water had to be drawn from a well for the farm animals and also for the family's drinking, cooking, and bathing needs.

But life on Barbados wasn't all work. Shirls and her sisters, along with cousins, enjoyed romps on the island, a paradise in young Shirls' eyes.

So many hot, sunny days.

Stunning white-sand beaches.

Clear-clear turquoise water.

Palm trees sent swaying by a breeze.

Life in Barbados continued to be a paradise in Shirls' eyes when, after a few years, Granny moved to a farm in a nearby village.

— ★ ★ ★ —

Back in Brooklyn, Shirls' working, working, *working* parents weren't making much headway. And they were not alone. Hard times had hit, kicked off by the stock market crash in October 1929. This was the start of the Great Depression.

With the rapid shuttering of banks and other businesses, from factories to mom-and-pop grocery stores, in 1933 about 25 percent of the workforce was out of a job. That was more than 15 million people.

President Franklin Delano Roosevelt, who took the oath of office on March 4, 1933, quickly acted to improve the economy. For example, he created federal agencies that provided jobs in construction, forestry, education, and other fields. Still, the Great Depression would drag on until 1939.

Despite the hard times, despite being a long way from owning a brownstone, despite having another mouth to feed (daughter Selma, born in fall 1931), after several long years of being apart from Muriel, Odessa, and Shirls, Ruby and Charles decided to bring their girls home.

When nine-year-old Shirls returned to Brooklyn, home was nothing like a paradise.

CHAPTER 3

OUR PLACES IN THE WORLD

WHEN RUBY ST. HILL BROUGHT HER GIRLS BACK TO
the States in May 1934 aboard the S.S. *Nerissa*, home was in Brownsville,
Brooklyn.

Even before the Great Depression, Brownsville was a high-crime,
high-poverty neighborhood, with a large population of Jewish
immigrants. People like Gita and Charles Kazin, whose son, Alfred,
became a celebrated writer.

Born about 10 years before Shirls, Alfred Kazin remembered
Brownsville as "New York's rawest, remotest, cheapest ghetto."

With its junkyards and lumberyards, its sweatshops, butcher shops,
liquor stores, pool halls, rundown wooden tenements, delicatessens,
peddlers and pushcarts, Brownsville, said Kazin, had a "damp sadness"
to it. The shrieks of factory whistles and the rattle and roll of the elevated
train made up some of the soundtrack of Brownsville lives.

Shirls and her family lived at 110 Liberty Avenue, in a four-room
railroad flat. "Like the cars on a train," she recalled, "the rooms were in a
line and you had to go through one to reach the next one. You came into
the kitchen, went on through two bedrooms, and arrived at the parlor in
the back."

It was a cold-water flat at that.

No running hot water meant boiling pots of water for baths. Come winter, the kitchen's coal stove was the sole source of heating. Shirls and her sisters sometimes huddled together all day in bed beneath who knows how many blankets or quilts. Under all that bedding perhaps a shivering, teeth-chattering Shirls daydreamed of hot, sunny days, white-sand beaches, clear-clear turquoise water, and palm trees sent swaying by a breeze.

★ ★ ★

In that cold-water flat, in that neighborhood of damp sadness, Mummy did some serious home training—likely from table manners to good hygiene—that would render her girls proper young ladies: "poised, modest, accomplished, educated, and graceful, prepared to take our places in the world," remembered Shirls.

And absolutely they were to be good Christians. On Sundays, they spent practically *all* day in church.

11:00 a.m. worship service.

2:30 p.m. Bible study.

7:30 p.m. worship service again.

Those three trips were to a Brethren church, a denomination Shirls described as being similar to the Religious Society of Friends, or Quakers.

At Shirls' church, there was no formal service, no high and exalted minister in charge. Congregants gathered in a large empty room on benches. Worship included long stretches of silence. That drove Shirls and her sisters nuts!

Another bummer: Hymns were sung unaccompanied by musical instruments because they were considered improper for a worship service.

While Mummy (like Granny) was strict-strict, Papa often urged her to cut their daughters some slack. "Ruby," he'd say, "you must remember these are American kids, not island kids."

Shirls also remembered that Papa was a fanatical reader.

Books.

Two or three newspapers some days.

"Papa read everything within reach. If he saw a man passing out handbills, he would cross the street to get one and read it."

Papa was also a "tireless talker." Many a night as she lay in bed she listened to him talking with friends around his kitchen table about current events of the day, much of it about labor unions.

Mr. St. Hill was proud-proud of being a union man, a member of the Bakery and Confectionery Workers International Union of America. When elected shop steward, the person who represents workers during talks with management, it was as if he'd been elected president of the United States. "He had to have his shoes shined and wear a tie when he went to union meetings," remembered Shirls.

And, oh, how Papa idolized Marcus Garvey, the Jamaican activist, journalist, and entrepreneur who in 1914 launched what eventually became the Universal Negro Improvement Association (UNIA). UNIA had about a thousand branches in the States, the Caribbean, Central America, and Africa by the time Shirls' parents emigrated. Garvey was a Moses to millions of Black people around the world with his calls to take pride in the African in them.

Papa instilled that same pride in his daughters and constantly urged them to excel.

You must make something of yourselves.

God gave you a brain; use it.

When Shirls returned to the States, people at Brownsville's Public School 84 took a somewhat dim view of her brain. While her reading and writing skills got a thumbs-up, her grasp of U.S. geography and history—

horrible. However much of a whiz she may have been on British history and the geography of Britain and the West Indies—that didn't count. Instead of entering the sixth grade as she expected, Shirls was held back, plopped into a class with kids *two years* younger than her.

Shirls was not a happy camper.

She lobbed spitballs.

She snapped rubber bands.

"Luckily someone diagnosed the trouble and did something about it," she later wrote: "a tutor in American geography and history for a year and a half, until I caught up with and passed my age-grade level."

Shirls had been lobbing spitballs and snapping rubber bands out of maddening boredom. What the school had discovered was that the girl had a near-genius IQ.

★ ★ ★

Brainy Shirls, who had returned to Brooklyn with a lilt in her voice that she would never lose, was about 12 when her family moved to 420 Ralph Avenue. Home was another four-room apartment, but the rooms were larger and the place had running hot water.

Steam heat too.

This was in a neighborhood that had once been two mostly white ones: Bedford Corners and Stuyvesant Heights.

Bedford Corners, once the more affluent one, had been home to lots of gorgeous single-family three- and four-story brownstones and whitestones.

Stuyvesant Heights, east of Bedford Corners, had mostly more modest housing, much of it apartments above stores.

When Shirls' family moved to the area, it was known as Bedford-Stuyvesant and as the even shorter "Bed-Stuy," a place where more and more Black people would live.

Just like when it came to jobs, being Black in Brooklyn generally meant being able to rent or buy only the least desirable housing. Many white landlords with property in certain neighborhoods refused to rent to Black people. Many white homeowners in some neighborhoods refused to sell their homes to Black people. As more and more Black people—a lot from the South and many from Harlem—moved to Bed-Stuy, more and more whites fled the neighborhood.

As the Great Depression wore on, more than a few Bed-Stuy homeowners who were struggling financially turned their single-family homes into apartments for two or more families. Other row houses and brownstones became boardinghouses for people who couldn't afford an apartment, just a room. More people in a row house or brownstone meant more wear and tear on the place.

In some cases, where brownstones or row houses remained single-family dwellings, owners who wanted to renovate and improve their property had a hard time getting bank loans because banks deemed their neighborhood a "bad" area, and so a loan was too risky.

A few years after the St. Hill family moved to the area, much of the Stuy in Bed-Stuy was labeled a slum. And soon, about 66 percent of Black Brooklynites would be living in Bed-Stuy.

★ ★ ★

Shirls' parents kept *working, working, working*. Now Papa worked at Brooklyn's Hygrade Bag Company, a factory that made burlap sacks widely used for storing and transporting all manner of things, from onions to coffee beans. Papa had changed jobs thinking he'd earn more money.

Didn't happen.

Before long he was working only two days a week and bringing home less than $20 a week.

He eventually got more hours at Hygrade, and at the end of a workday he was thoroughly worn out, as were his hands. Shirls remembered them as "rough and callused from the tons of rough burlap he carried."

But until Papa started making more money, Mummy got a job in another part of Brooklyn, Flatbush, as a domestic worker for well-to-do white people.

Enter Shirls-in-Charge.

★ ★ ★ ★ ★ ★ ★ ★ ★

CHAPTER 4

HAD TO READ

"BY THE TIME I WAS TWO AND A HALF," SHIRLS LATER
bragged, "I was already dominating other children around me—with
my mouth."

It would be reported later in her life that when she was four an
astrologer predicted that she'd be "a leader of her people."

Papa said amen to that. "He believed in me. He said I'd be a great
woman," she once told a reporter. She remembered her dad telling her,
"I know you have it, Shirls. That road will be tough, but you'll do it."

★ ★ ★

Back in the 1930s, when school lunch was not the norm, Shirls-in-Charge
meant that on school days come noon she left her junior high school to
pick up her sisters at their elementary school—about a 10-minute walk
if she dashed.

Next, a short walk home for lunch, most days a glass of milk and
"a bun."

After lunch, bossy Shirls scooted her sisters back to their school, then
hustled on to hers. When school let out, she hurried back to fetch them,
then headed home.

Straight home and stayed there.

There was no ripping and running in the streets. The St. Hill girls had
to do their homework and always—

"We had to read."

Books that had been Christmas presents, like a Nancy Drew or Bobbsey Twins adventure.

Books that had perhaps been birthday presents too.

Books checked out every other Saturday when Mummy marched them to their local library.

But as in Barbados, Shirls' life in Brooklyn wasn't all work and no play. When the weather was warm Mummy sometimes treated them to picnics at Coney Island, for example. Also, now and then the girls got to go to a party.

Given Mummy's sewing skills, the St. Hill girls were always stylishly dressed at those parties. They were also often the butt of jokes because they were the first to arrive and the first to leave.

Shirls remembered that just when a party "got going and I was starting to enjoy dancing"—perhaps doing the Charleston or the Lindy Hop—her sister Odessa spoiled it all by playing party cop. "You remember what Mummy said. We've been here an hour and it's time to go home."

With all that discipline, all that reading, all that prodding to amount to something—not to mention her near-genius IQ—Shirls landed a spot at Bed-Stuy's Girls' High School, which was about 50 percent white.

At a time when many people, regardless of race or ethnicity, didn't want to live in Bed-Stuy, many were thrilled to have their daughters attend Girls' High. As public high schools went, it had always been one of the best in the nation.

— ★ ★ ★ —

When Shirls started high school in September 1939, the world was in chaos and crisis. On September 1, Nazi Germany had invaded Poland, marking the start of World War II.

At first Britain and France led the fight against Germany, Japan, and Italy, all standing for fascism, tyranny, dictatorships—standing against democracy.

Early on, the United States supplied Britain and France with weapons, tanks, and other military equipment. The country didn't officially enter the war until December 8, 1941, the day after Japanese pilots pulled off an astounding attack on the U.S. naval base at Pearl Harbor on Hawaii's Oahu island.

Before and after the United States entered the war, Shirls' world swirled with frightening banner headlines.

"GERMANS OCCUPY PARIS, PRESS ON SOUTH ..."

"BRITISH BOMB BERLIN ..."

"NAZIS ADVANCE IN YUGOSLAVIA ..."

"SUBMARINE SHELLS CALIFORNIA OIL PLANT ..."

★ ★ ★

Scary, scary days. Days of air-raid drills, of hunts for spies and saboteurs, of occasional dimouts and blackouts, of manned antiaircraft guns at New York forts, of the rationing of sugar, meat, and other goods.

As for Shirls, she more than soldiered on at Girls' High.

She excelled in French, earning a medal. What's more, Shirls was vice president of the Junior Arista honor society.

★ ★ ★

"Arista" derives from the Greek word for "best." And when Shirls graduated from Girls' High in 1942, she had options on where to go next to be her best. She had snagged several scholarships. Two really thrilled her.

One was for Vassar College, some 90 miles away up in Poughkeepsie,

New York. This prestigious, private, then all-women's school had only recently begun admitting Black women. Knowingly, that is. Years earlier several very light-skinned Black women had attended Vassar passing as white.

The other scholarship was for Oberlin College, in Oberlin, Ohio, nearly 500 miles away. It was one of the first U.S. colleges to admit Black people and women (back in the 1830s).

Vassar or Oberlin? Vassar or Oberlin? Vassar or—

Neither.

Those scholarships didn't cover room and board, expenses Shirls' parents couldn't afford—parents who by then had the family living in a small apartment building at 316 Patchen Avenue in Bed-Stuy. Home was now a six-room apartment. It was rent free because Papa was the building's janitor.

Even if Ruby and Charles had the dough for room and board at Vassar or Oberlin, given the tight rein Mummy kept on her girls, it's doubtful that Shirls would have been allowed to go away to college, not some 90 miles away and certainly not nearly 500 miles away. Instead, Shirls went to a school that she could reach initially by subway and trolley car: Brooklyn College.

Located in the largely Jewish, mostly middle-class neighborhood of Midwood, it was a college for which the price of admission was a GPA of at least 83.5 for women and 79 for men and passage of a rigorous entrance exam. It was also a school where Shirls would be one of only about 60 Black students among its nearly 14,000 undergraduate and graduate students.

★ ★ ★

When Shirls entered Brooklyn College, she was set to become a teacher. "There was no other road open to a young black woman," she later claimed. "Law, medicine, even nursing were too expensive."

Yes, in the 1940s the doors of opportunity were far from wide open to young Black women, but more than a few didn't wait for doors to open. They knocked them down.

Dominating other kids when she was a kid was one thing. So was being Shirls-in-Charge of her sisters on school days. Defying norms was another thing altogether. She did not yet have it in her to push back against society's ideas about what a Black woman could do, did not yet have the guts to make a road, forge a path, blaze any kind of trail. Fight.

To be an attorney, physician, or an entrepreneur.

Or to pursue her passion: acting.

From a young age, Shirls loved to dance. "I come alive on a dance floor," she gloried years later. "I'm very creative. I use my hands and my body. Even now I amaze people when I dance." Young Shirls was also quite the piano player. While saving up for a house, her parents had scraped together money for a piano and piano lessons. Along the way, Shirls also picked up the gift of mimicry.

Had Shirls set out to be an actress, Mummy would have been mortified. Papa probably wouldn't have been too pleased either. It simply wasn't the sort of thing a proper young Bajan woman did. Teaching most definitely was.

So with the goal of becoming a teacher, off went Shirls to Brooklyn College, where she began, she said, to "bump up against more of the world."

★ ★ ★ ★ ★ ★ ★ ★ ★ ★

CHAPTER 5

ALIVE WITH ACTIVITY

BROOKLYN COLLEGE WAS A WONDERLAND OF TREES,

from American elms to silverbells. Along with its stately brick buildings, splendid athletic field, and lovely lily pond, those trees made the school, said a reporter, one of the "miracles in a metropolis supposedly victim to cement and brick."

The college was in the business of miracles. Sort of. It was created as a way for young women and men from working-class families to rise in life, especially white immigrants and their sons and daughters. That's why the college was initially tuition free. And Shirls remembered the place as being "alive with activity."

Posters and flyers plastered around campus advertised guest speakers on an array of pressing issues—from the jailing of trade unionists and the persecution of Jewish people in Europe to racial injustice in the United States.

During these fraught and fractious days Shirls applied herself to more than her coursework. She, too, was alive with activity.

Shirls joined the Harriet Tubman Society, which lobbied the college for courses in Black history.

Shirls was also a member of Ipothia, a social club she started with other Black women students. Ipothia, open to non-Black women too, stood for "In Pursuit of the Highest in All." It was devoted to self-improvement on all fronts, from ethics to academics.

Apparently keen on fruitful relationships with Spanish-speaking students and eager to learn about Latin America, Shirls joined the Pan-American club.

This star on the college debate team was also a member of the political science club. When attending lectures by some of its white guest speakers—supposedly liberal, progressive people—Shirls got a lot of shocks. Some "looked at my people as another breed, less human than they." These speakers said things like, "We've got to help the Negro because the Negro is limited."

One of those speakers was Brooklynite Stan Steingut, a future New York State lawmaker. In a talk he insisted that Black people couldn't get ahead, make any real progress without white people—didn't have the right stuff for leadership.

"Uh huh—that's what you think," Shirls said to herself.

While in college Shirls also summoned up the guts to take on the sexism binding the student council, all male by tradition. The two times when young white women dared to run for president, Shirls sprang into action. "I painted posters, helped write slogans and speeches, helped organize rallies and spoke at them myself."

Shirls spread her wings outside of Brooklyn College. She joined the Brooklyn chapter of the National Association for the Advancement of Colored People (NAACP), a leading civil rights organization. She was much more involved with another major civil rights organization, the Urban League. Shirls' volunteer work for its Brooklyn chapter included teaching arts and crafts at its community center.

★ ★ ★

While Shirls was thriving at Brooklyn College, her parents had continued their striving. After years of toil, years of scrimping and saving, some 20 years after they immigrated to the United States, in 1945 the St. Hill family, at last, had a home of their own: 1094 Prospect Place.

It wasn't a soaring Victorian brownstone, but it was close: a limestone two-story row house with a street-level basement. Located on one of Bed-Stuy's nicer blocks, that home cost $10,000, roughly $144,000 in today's dollars.

The purchase was indeed, as Shirls later wrote, "a really remarkable achievement for parents of four children, who started with nothing and lived through the depression on a laborer's and a domestic's pay."

As for Shirls, a sociology major with a minor in Spanish, she was still intent on becoming a teacher. But oddly she took not one education course. In any event, when she graduated from Brooklyn College with honors in 1946 (and with World War II over), Shirls geared up to take her place in the world.

What an uphill battle that was!

Some schools turned her down when she showed up for an interview and the interviewer saw that she was Black. Regardless of the interviewer's race or ethnicity, having no education courses certainly didn't help her case.

Neither did her size. Though going on 22, at about 5 feet 4 inches tall and weighing 90 pounds Shirls looked like a teenager. "I didn't look old enough to teach, and most of the interviewers told me so."

Day after day, Shirls went job hunting.

School after school turned her down.

One day a fed-up, frustrated Shirls fought back. "At least you could try me!" she exploded. "Put me on as a probationer! Give me a chance to show you! Give me a chance to find out whether I can do the job … don't judge me by my size."

Fighting back paid off. Eula Hodges, head of Mt. Calvary Child Care Center in Harlem, gave Shirls a shot.

Convinced that teaching would be her life's work, before her trial period at Mt. Calvary was up and the day care center took her on as a teacher's aide, Shirls went back to school. This time she went across the East River for evening classes at Columbia University's Teachers College. There she began work on a master's degree in early childhood education.

While holding down a day job and going to night school, Shirls, much to her surprise, fell in love.

———— ★ ★ ★ ————

She was at Columbia one evening when a peaceful, stocky, good-looking Jamaican man, Conrad Quintin Chisholm, "stopped and persuaded me to stand still long enough to get acquainted."

Conrad, eight years older than Shirls, had a heck of a time doing that. She had sworn off men after one broke her heart.

During her senior year of college Shirls had fallen big-time for this guy whom she met when working at a jewelry factory in Manhattan during Easter break.

Like Conrad, he was older, also handsome, also Jamaican. One lunch date led to more dates and eventually to an engagement. But then Shirls discovered that her fiancé, whose name she never revealed to the public, was a scoundrel.

He had a wife and children in Jamaica. He was also a crook—"up to his eyebrows in an immigration fraud racket." For that, he was arrested, then deported.

Shirls was shattered by his betrayal.

Couldn't sleep. Couldn't eat. "I gradually became a skeleton."

To rescue their devastated daughter, Ruby and Charles St. Hill heeded a doctor's advice and sent her to live with friends on a farm in New Jersey.

Bit by bit, thanks to good old country air, good old country quiet, good old country home cooking, and that Jersey family's love, Shirls pushed back to strength. "I groped my way back to reality."

This reality would be a life devoted to the well-being of children.

No room for boyfriends!

No room for a husband!

But then came the persistent Conrad Quintin Chisholm.

Born in Montego Bay, Jamaica, calm Conrad was a decent, hardworking man who had immigrated to the States in the 1940s. He started his New York City life working in Manhattan's garment district, then at an Automat as a short-order cook. He'd eventually become a private investigator for insurance companies.

Shirls' attempts to drive Conrad away—"glacial aloofness, standing him up, angry sarcasm, avoiding him"—failed. His "calm determination and his inexhaustible sympathy got through to me." In fall 1949 the couple married, having a pretty big West Indian–style wedding.

By then, Shirls had been up to more than working, attending night school, and falling in love again.

She had become alive to politics.

TWO THINGS

"YOU OUGHT TO GO INTO POLITICS."

That was Louis Warsoff back when Shirls was in college. Warsoff, a political science professor, had just seen her give an amazing performance in a debating match.

Warsoff was the most progressive white man she had ever met. And she loved him for that. But when "Proffy," as she called him, suggested she pursue politics, Shirls thought he was out of his mind.

"Proffy," she said, "you forget two things. I'm black—and I'm a woman."

But Shirls did have a political itch. To scratch it, while still in college, she began checking out the Democratic Club of the 17th Assembly District (AD).

The 17th AD was a majority-Black district that included Bed-Stuy, but it was controlled by white men. When it came to the district's Democratic Party, it was mostly Irishmen who did that controlling.

Controlled who got jobs at the post office, for example, when slots opened up.

Controlled who got supported for elective office, say, for a judgeship or to represent the district in the New York State Assembly in Albany. (That is the lower house in the New York State Legislature, a state equivalent to Congress's House of Representatives.)

And definitely these Irishmen controlled who got to be the party's district leader—that is, the Boss.

When Shirls began checking out the 17th AD Democratic Club, a short walk from her home, the party's district leader was Steve Carney. Like other politicians, "Boss Carney" doled out free fresh turkeys as Thanksgiving neared and Christmas baskets a month later. But when it came to the needs, the concerns, of Black folks in his district—

"He is conspicuously absent from programs held in the district to promote civic, religious, and other forms of progress," complained New York City's *Amsterdam News*, a major Black-owned newspaper. It was also upset with Carney for overlooking Black people when it came to fixing folks up with jobs.

Carney needed to go!

The *Amsterdam News* reminded its readers that a group of Black people had mounted a campaign for the 17th AD to have a Black leader.

We don't know if Shirls, months out of college, was part of that effort (which didn't succeed), but when she attended the twice-a-week meetings at the clubhouse, she definitely witnessed Carney's disrespect for Black people. It ticked her off to see Carney sitting "with his flunkies on a dais at the far end of the room, while the voters came in and took high-backed chairs to wait their turns for an audience."

Perhaps someone had been served with an eviction notice, lost a job, or had a son (or daughter) in a spot of trouble with the law.

During one meeting Shirls asked why sanitation trucks didn't roll through Bed-Stuy as often as they did through some white neighborhoods.

"Such questions were unwelcome," she recalled. But that didn't stop her from speaking up, speaking out.

Shirls became even more alive to politics after she met the Democrat Wesley McDonald "Mac" Holder. Like Shirls' papa, this native of present-day Guyana idolized Marcus Garvey.

A former editor of the *Amsterdam News*, Holder was a statistician by trade, working at the Brooklyn District Attorney's Office. Shirls later called him the "shrewdest, toughest, and hardest-working political animal in Brooklyn, probably in New York City, and maybe elsewhere." Like others in Brooklyn and around the nation, he was on a mission for Black communities to have Black elected officials.

While under his wing, Shirls began to earn the equivalent of a college degree in politics. At the same time, she was also learning the ropes by continuing to work within the 17th AD Democratic Club.

Her early work with that club included decorating cigar boxes used to collect money and hold raffle tickets during the club's annual fundraiser, a card party.

Before she decorated those cigar boxes, Shirls had to first beg them up from local shops. Other club women, often politicians' wives, who organized the card party, had to bring out the begging bowls too. Money for prizes. Money to get raffle tickets printed up. Money for the whole shebang. And at the end of the day, men controlled the proceeds.

Ridiculous!, thought Shirls. "Why should we put up with it?" she one day asked the women, putting a bug in their ears to stand up for themselves. Sure enough, during one clubhouse meeting a woman asked about being given a budget to work with.

"Women are the backbone of this club, and you know it," Shirls chimed in.

The meeting was declared out of order.

"It will stay out of order until you start to pay attention to us," declared another woman.

That year the women were given $700 to mount the fundraiser that raked in more than $8,000.

Shirls' reputation as a troublemaker was cemented. And she kept on speaking up, speaking out, kept on watching and learning the ins and outs of politics.

★ ★ ★

In 1953 Shirley Chisholm, then in her late 20s, got on board with a serious challenge to the white political machine: Holder's campaign for Brooklyn to have a Black judge. His candidate was Lewis Flagg, Jr., former chief counsel for the NAACP's Brooklyn branch. Flagg was running for the 17th AD's seat on the municipal court bench.

Shirley and Holder's other foot soldiers worked overtime getting out the vote for Flagg.

In the Democratic primary Flagg barely squeaked out a victory—by 75 votes—over Judge Benjamin H. Schor, a white man.

In November's general election, Schor, who then ran on the Liberal Party ticket, got 6,332 votes. Black attorney William H. Staves, the Republican candidate, got 10,332 votes.

With 25,913 votes, Flagg became Brooklyn's first Black judge.

★ ★ ★

Holder soon capitalized on Flagg's victory by forming a new political club: the Bedford-Stuyvesant Political League (BSPL), of which he was elected president. Unopposed. Just the way he liked it.

In 1954 the BSPL ran Black candidates for a number of offices, including for the New York State Legislature and for the U.S. Congress, but none of them won. Still, the BSPL kept fighting.

Shirley kept fighting with it.

Starting in January 1956, she did that fighting as the BSPL's first vice president. And in months to come, the name "Shirley Chisholm" was in the news more and more.

As a vice president of the 17th AD Democratic Club in January 1957.

In January 1958, as one of six women the Women's Council of Brooklyn celebrated for outstanding community service at its annual breakfast.

Later that year the *Amsterdam News* reported that Shirley was heading a fundraiser for the Stuyvesant Community Center. Run by and for Black people, the center served roughly 1,500 children.

It was also in 1958 that Shirley had a big bust-up with Mac Holder.

———— ★ ★ ★ ————

Having been a good soldier—having stuffed her share of envelopes, rung her share of doorbells—Shirley thought, "Why not me?" when it came to the BSPL presidency.

Holder was furious. He blasted her for that.

She shot back that "there was nothing in the League's constitution that said he was supposed to be president for life." She refused to back down, feeling strongly that she "had a right to run. That was what democracy was all about."

Never expecting to win, Shirley exercised that right.

And was trounced.

The defeat took some of the fight out of Shirley, caused her to step back from political activity.

———— ★ ★ ★ ————

By then, Shirley had long since earned that master's degree and been licensed to teach. She had been director of Friend in Need, a private day care center in Brooklyn. From there, she had moved on to the

Hamilton-Madison Child Care Center, located in the shadow of the Brooklyn Bridge, on Manhattan's Lower East Side. Hamilton-Madison served more than 100 Black and Puerto Rican children.

As its director, Shirley had a lot to be in charge of, overseeing a staff that included 24 teachers. And she was definitely the boss—a tough cookie!

That didn't always end well.

She hurt people's feelings.

She ruffled feathers.

One woman remembered her as "often unfair." But, said the woman, Shirley "learned from her mistakes." She summed her up as a "shrewd cookie."

In December 1959 this shrewd cookie went to work for the City Division of Day Care, then part of New York City's Bureau of Child Welfare (now the Administration for Children's Services). In this job, Shirley had oversight of 10 day care centers. That meant supervising 126 people, from directors and teachers to maintenance workers. She was also in charge of a budget of $397,000, more than $3 million in today's dollars.

Shirley's job kept her plenty busy and on the move—visiting the centers, attending conferences, going to meetings. Some of those meetings were with community leaders, where Shirley, prone to rapid-fire speech, worked hard to drive home the point that the city needed not just more day care centers but top-quality ones.

Day care wasn't just a problem in New York City. In November 1959 a newspaper reported that this problem involved three million mothers and seven million children under the age of 12 around the nation. The majority of children whose mothers worked outside the home were minded by relatives, while roughly 400,000 had to take care of themselves after school.

While Shirley was fighting for more and better day care centers, she was, as she put it, "drawn back into politics."

CHAPTER 7

BATTLING FOR A BETTER BED-STUY

IN FEBRUARY 1960 SHIRLEY GOT BUSY WITH THE
relatively new Unity Democratic Club (UDC), another group of
reformers intent on getting Black representation for the 17th AD. Just
like Mac Holder's BSPL, the UDC would promote candidates from
within its ranks in its very ambitious goal, wrote Shirley, "to do what the
Bedford-Stuyvesant Political League had never managed to do: take over
the entire Seventeenth Assembly District political organization and boot
out the failing but still potent white machine."

The UDC's Bed-Stuy founders included social worker Ruth Goring,
who was, like Shirley, of Bajan descent. Another co-founder was attorney
Tom Jones, who served as the UDC's executive director. Like Shirley, this
World War II veteran had been a member of the BSPL and was the child
of Bajan immigrants. Small in stature, Jones had a commanding presence.

Later Black joiners of the interracial UDC included longtime civil
rights and political activist Jocelyn Cooper. Years earlier, Jocelyn had lit
a fire under her husband, Andy, to get politically active. And he did. He
joined the UDC in 1961 and would one day launch the *City Sun,* a
newspaper with the motto "Speaking Truth to Power." Well before that,

he would take some radical action that would pave the way for Shirley Chisholm to make history.

Back in October 1960, the UDC had a monster rally, the kickoff to a voter registration campaign. Jones told the *Amsterdam News* that he had some 50 people ready to hit the streets of Bed-Stuy and ring doorbell after doorbell to get folks registered. This was to help his bid for the Democratic nomination to represent the 17th AD in Albany and to be its district leader.

Jones was running against incumbent Sam Berman, a Jewish man who had been representing the district since 1954. And it was a district that had slid into more of a slum. Especially Bed-Stuy.

Crumbling schools.

Crummy housing.

Crime on the rise.

Some of that crime stemmed from street gang activity.

Some of it from the heroin epidemic that gripped New York City. Some addicts mugged people, robbed homes, shoplifted, and committed other crimes to get money for a "fix."

And when Jones ran for office, Bed-Stuy was a much more crowded place. Its population had swelled from about 250,000 in the 1930s to more than 400,000, with Blacks in the majority and with sizable populations of whites and Puerto Ricans. And so many of Bed-Stuy's people lived in poverty—or close to it.

With even more families crammed into once single-family homes and more people inhabiting its public housing complexes, garbage was also a big problem in Bed-Stuy.

Garbage overflowing in trash cans.

Garbage strewn in alleys.

Garbage piled high in abandoned lots.

Garbage hitting pavements via the "airmail express"—that is, tossed out windows. That's because in some blocks people struggling with drug addiction lurked in alleys where trash cans were kept. Also, many trash cans didn't have lids because they were often used as shields in street fights. Lidless garbage cans meant rats and cats poking around spoiled food, soiled diapers, and other trash inside those cans.

Who would want to go near that?

Thus the airmail express.

The blame for Bed-Stuy's garbage problem couldn't all be laid at the feet of drug addicts, lidless trash cans, rats, and cats. The sanitation system was flawed. When it came to garbage pickups and street cleaning, overcrowded Bed-Stuy got about the same service as Marine Park, an overwhelmingly white and much less densely populated neighborhood with mostly one- and two-family homes.

In a campaign ad Jones had vowed that he would "not rest" until his community had good schools, until all workers in it had a living wage, until his community had first-rate services, from health care to sanitation.

Shirley and her UDC colleagues weren't just thinking locally. They got behind the boycott against goods from South Africa because of apartheid. This was a brutal social, political, and economic system in which some 10.9 million Black people, roughly 1.5 million "coloureds" (mixed-race people), and 477,000 Indians—totaling 80 percent of the population—lived under white minority rule.

The UDC had also called for Brooklynites (and all Northerners) to boycott and picket F. W. Woolworth's five-and-dime stores until the chain ended Jim Crow policies in its southern stores. While these stores were happy to sell Black people everything from school supplies to bric-a-brac, Black people were banned from lunch counter swivel stools to enjoy, say, a 55-cent chicken salad sandwich or a 25-cent banana split.

The call for a boycott of Woolworth stores in the North was in sympathy with action taken in the South back on February 1, 1960: Four neatly dressed and respectful Black college students in Greensboro, North Carolina, staged a sit-in at the Woolworth on that city's South Elm Street. For months other college students did the same in the face of harassment from white people. These sit-ins ended in late July 1960 when Woolworth ended its whites-only lunch counter policy in all its stores.

★ ★ ★

Whether the issue was sanitation pickups, housing, or Jim Crow at home and abroad—

"We made a lot of noise," Shirley recalled.

But all that noise didn't result in a victory. On November 8, 1960, Berman beat Jones.

But Jones didn't give up.

And persistence paid off. On November 6, 1962, Jones, by then a district co-leader with Ruth Goring, became the 17th AD's first Black assembly person.

That same month, Shirley became a vice president of the Central Brooklyn Coordinating Council (CBCC). Formed in the late 1950s, the CBCC was a coalition of groups battling for a better Bed-Stuy.

The CBCC agenda Shirley drafted for 1963 included a fight for new and improved housing. Also, solutions to overcrowded classrooms, paltry programs for children with special needs, and low high school graduation rates.

In hopes of keeping kids and teens from dropping out of school, joining gangs, and doing other things that fall under the category of "juvenile delinquency," Shirley put on the want list local and federal funds for programs that would keep Bed-Stuy's young people out of trouble and on a positive path.

★ ★ ★

Work, work, *work*—or lack of it—was another serious problem. To combat the high unemployment rate, especially among Black and Puerto Rican people, in February 1963, Shirley was a member of a delegation that had a sit-down at City Hall with New York City mayor Robert Wagner. When Shirley and crew left, they had the mayor's yes to a Department of Labor service center in Bed-Stuy.

Among other things, this job center's mission was to help people find out about job openings and on-the-job training programs (in car repair, for example). It would also help people who dropped out of high school prepare for the General Educational Development (GED) test and get a certificate akin to a high school diploma.

★ ★ ★

That job center opened on Monday, July 1, 1963, in the heart of Bed-Stuy, at 1178 Fulton Street.

Some 500 people turned out in 90-degree heat for the ribbon-cutting ceremony—brass band and all—taking courage, taking heart, buoyed by Mayor Wagner's stirring words.

"The alarm bells have been sounded, North and South, for the government—all levels of government—to act and act now," he said. That action was "to remedy the conditions of discrimination, segregation and deprivation which have so long been the lot of so many of our fellow-Americans." Recent protests, the mayor added, offered "dramatic evidence of what might be called the Spirit of '63. It has been a militant spirit, a vigorous spirit, a fearless spirit."

While Shirley was in the trenches battling for a better Bed-Stuy, people around the nation were battling for a better, a more just, America.

That Spirit of 1963 was the spirit of the civil rights movement, and a lot had happened by then.

In 1955 longtime activist Rosa Parks had committed her famous act of resistance on a bus in Montgomery, Alabama, refusing to give up her seat to a white person. Her defiance sparked a bus boycott that lasted 381 days. It ended on December 20, 1956, with its number one spokesperson, the Reverend Dr. Martin Luther King, Jr., in the national spotlight. Most important, it ended with Montgomery's Jim Crow bus system outlawed by a court ruling.

In 1957, in the fall, nine courageous Black teens began to brave the physical and psychological brutality of white teens and adults in their mission to integrate Central High in Little Rock, Arkansas.

When in 1963 Shirley's mayor spoke of that militant, vigorous, fearless spirit, there had been lunch counter sit-ins—and not just in Greensboro, North Carolina—along with swim-ins and wade-ins at whites-only public beaches and pools, read-ins at whites-only public libraries, and pray-ins at white churches that didn't want Black people in their pews.

And the interracial Congress of Racial Equality (CORE) had launched the Freedom Rides, in which Black and white northern activists boarded buses heading south to test rulings that banned Jim Crow on interstate buses and in bus terminals.

There had been great resistance from white people to these and other calls for the end of segregation, the end of Black people being relegated to second-class citizenship—calls for social justice.

For example, on January 14, 1963, on the steps of the Alabama State Capitol, newly elected Governor George Wallace declared in his inaugural address, "Segregation now ... segregation tomorrow ... segregation forever."

Months later, in June, in Jackson, Mississippi, a white supremacist shot dead Black World War II veteran Medgar Evers, chief of the NAACP's Mississippi branch. Evers was returning home from a civil rights rally, walking from his car to his home.

When he was shot, Evers's "bundle of T-shirts, emblazoned 'Jim Crow Must Go' fell to the ground," reported New York's *Daily News*.

But in spite of that resistance, millions remained sustained by that militant spirit, that vigorous spirit, that fearless spirit.

Two months after Bed-Stuy got that job center, on August 28, 1963, roughly a quarter-million people turned out in the nation's capital for the March on Washington for Jobs and Freedom.

The year marked the hundredth anniversary of the Emancipation Proclamation, the decree President Abraham Lincoln issued during the Civil War, which led to the end of slavery in the United States. Now, in August 1963, in this massive march, people called for fuller freedom for Black people—freedom from Jim Crow—and wider opportunities.

Shirley wasn't at this epic event, but she penned a poem in its honor, "Freedom March."

"Freedom March" told of people heading to D.C. "from every corner of this gigantic land" to "make a firm stand."

Both young and old and black
and white
Came through the piercing
stillness of night ...

Shirley wrote of gospel great Mahalia Jackson "crying out of her soul / In spiritual language—so deep and so bold."

Shirley also saluted some of the day's speakers, including labor leader A. Philip Randolph "with bearing so proud" and Martin Luther King, Jr., "the giant of them all."

★ ★ ★

Eighteen days later, members of a white hate group, the Ku Klux Klan, bombed the 16th Street Baptist Church in Birmingham, Alabama, killing four girls and wounding more than a dozen other people.

In the wake of the church bombing, Shirley and others had reason to keep on hoping.

Back in June 1963, President John F. Kennedy (JFK) had announced that he was sending Congress a civil rights bill aimed at killing Jim Crow. But then ...

On November 22, there was reason to despair, weep, and mourn.

The nation, the world, reeled from newsflashes of JFK's assassination. It happened as his motorcade cruised through Dealey Plaza in downtown Dallas, Texas.

Eight days later, the *Amsterdam News* reported that Assemblyman Jones called on the people of Bed-Stuy, people around the nation, to put a lit candle or white light in their windows every evening for a week.

Shirley was among Bed-Stuy's community leaders who pledged to promote the "Lighted Candle" memorial to JFK.

What would the Spirit of 1964 bring?

For the nation?

For New York City?

For Brooklyn?

For Bed-Stuy?

For Shirley Chisholm?

CHAPTER 8

KEY WOMAN

YOU OUGHT TO GO INTO POLITICS.

By 1964 Proffy's prod didn't strike Shirley as one bit ridiculous.

When Tom Jones decided to run for a local judgeship, Shirley put herself forward to be the UDC's candidate for his New York State Assembly seat.

People began fighting Shirley on this. People outside the UDC and people within it—especially men who were themselves considering a run. They were men, she said, who "didn't want to see me in a position of any more importance than I already had."

Tough! That was Shirley's attitude.

She believed with all her heart that she deserved a shot at elective office.

Deserved it because she had *earned* it.

"By then," remembered Shirley, "I had spent about ten years in ward politics and had done everything else but run for office. Starting as a cigar box decorator, I had compiled voter lists, carried petitions, rung doorbells, manned the telephone, stuffed envelopes, and helped voters get to the polls. I had done it all to help other people get elected."

Her time had come, she felt, to not just support change-makers but to be one.

And she faced things with courage. To the UDC's executive committee she said this: "If you need to have a discussion, have a discussion. But it makes no difference to me. I intend to fight."

On April 27, 1964, Shirley was officially on the ballot for the upcoming June primary in which voters would decide which Democrat—her or Black attorney Harold Brady—would face off against the candidates of other parties in November.

On May 9 page one of the *Amsterdam News* Brooklyn edition had a headshot of Shirley, titled, in thick black lettering, "Pioneer." For the first time in Brooklyn's history, the Democratic Party had a woman running for the 17th AD's seat in Albany.

The *Amsterdam News* mentioned Shirley's excellent schooling and her sterling career in education. It ticked off some of her honors and awards. The paper included her 1963 award for community service from the Key Women of America, an organization of Black women all about community service and Black advancement. By the time she ran for the assembly seat, she was the chapter's president.

Also by then, Shirley was one of Brooklyn's most stylish and, at times, flamboyant dressers. For example, back in February 1964, at a Sunday afternoon tea for a senior citizen home, Shirley was, said a reporter, "stunning in a black velvet chapeau, trimmed in brilliantes and feathers, and an impeccable mink trimmed black Persian lamb [coat]."

While she loved her finery, Shirley was still very much a woman of the people. While running for that assembly seat, she was just as at ease talking to folks on street corners and stoops and in public housing complexes as she was at a tea or a garden party.

And when it came to the people, it was the votes of women that Shirley most coveted, for she had done the math: The 17th AD had roughly 5,000 more registered women voters than men voters.

Black women—that's the group Shirley especially rallied to her side. "Elect me to dramatize the problems of black women," she said to them.

Those problems included inadequate day care, low-paying jobs, and lack of affordable health care.

But Shirley didn't write off men, though getting their support often took some fight. Back when she was gathering signatures to get on the ballot, an elderly gent chided her with this: "Young woman, what are you doing out here in this cold?" Had she fixed her husband breakfast that morning? Had she tidied her house? "What are you doing running for office? That is something for men."

"I handled all such hecklers, male and female, the same way," Shirley later wrote. "I told them calmly that I had been serving the community for a number of years and now I would appreciate an opportunity to serve it on a higher level, in elected office."

By the way, that elderly gent signed her petition.

★ ★ ★

On June 2, 1964, Shirley won the Democratic primary over Harold Brady, 4,290 to 1,729. Next up: the general election.

It would be a three-way race. Both Shirley's opponents were Black men. One was the Liberal Party's Simeon Golar, a city attorney. The other was Republican Charles Lewis, pastor of Canaan Baptist Church.

And Shirley had a problem: "what to run my campaign with."

While the UDC had no shortage of volunteers to distribute flyers, get out mailings, and such, it didn't have big bucks then. With Conrad's blessing, Shirley dipped into their savings for a total of $4,000 (about $33,000 in today's dollars) to cover the cost of printing those flyers, posting those mailings, renting hall space for rallies, and everything else it takes to mount a campaign.

Along with Conrad, Shirley had Key Women by her side, not

surprisingly. "We all got out and pitched for her," recalled member Constance Rose. "We went with petitions and everything. We were actually her backbone."

While Shirley was working to have her own victory, she was, no doubt, really eager to see a new law of the land have a victory, too, one that would be a big win for the civil rights movement.

★ ★ ★

After the assassination of JFK, his vice president and successor, Lyndon B. Johnson (LBJ), championed a civil rights bill that was mightier than the slain president's. LBJ's bill made it flat-out illegal to engage in discrimination when it came to schooling, places of accommodations such as restaurants, parks, and pools, as well as in the workplace. This sweeping bill passed the U.S. House of Representatives in February 1964.

When Shirley beat Brady in June, the U.S. Senate still had not voted on the bill. But she and other civil rights activists had reason for hope.

There was also hope that the nation would make a serious effort to lift millions of Americans out of poverty. At the time, roughly 36 million Americans—about 20 percent of the population—lived in poverty.

Every hue and creed.

In the countryside, in cities.

So many were senior citizens.

Shirley and others had reason to hope for help for such folks because in early 1964, in his State of the Union address, LBJ had announced an "unconditional war" on poverty: "Our aim is not only to relieve the symptom of poverty, but to cure it and, above all, to prevent it." Months later, during a commencement speech at the University of Michigan, he called on the graduates, the faculty—all Americans—to join him in

"the battle to build the Great Society," a nation that took better care
of its people.

★ ★ ★

It was also in 1964 that more and more people joined the civil
rights crusade. For example, hundreds committed to the miracle of
Freedom Summer when activists from the South and North engaged
in a massive voter education and registration drive among Black people
in Mississippi. For decades that state's white power structure, like others
in the South, kept legions of Black people from voting. They used
intimidation. They used violence. They also made it difficult in various
ways for Black people to register to vote. One was a literacy test—proof
of a certain level of ability in reading and writing. So often Black people
were given tests that were much harder than those given to white people.

Up north the fight for social justice was also strong. For example, on
Monday, February 3, roughly 360,000 of New York City's one million
public school children played hooky for a cause: a protest against lousy
schools. Many of these mostly Black and Puerto Rican girls and boys
joined their parents and other adults in picket lines. One chant was
"Jim Crow Must Go!"

Months later, on June 19, hope was again in the air. The Senate finally
passed the civil rights bill. And on July 2, 1964, LBJ signed that landmark
bill into law.

And Shirley had another poem, "Law of the Land."

In celebrating the Civil Rights Act of 1964, she declared that on
July 2, 1964, when "the temperature was high, and tempers were hot,"
300 years of "toil and strife" had come to an end. She had faith that "True
Americans" would "rise to the task" of building on this new law of the
land—of doing all in their power to get the nation to live up to its creed.

She ended on a very hopeful note:

Our preachments of democracy
will now ring true
O'er the wide, wide world and
the oceans blue.

Two weeks after this new law of the land was signed, on July 16, when the temperature in New York City was high, tempers flared in Harlem and a riot broke out. This was in the wake of the killing of a Black teen: 15-year-old James Powell, shot twice by a white off-duty cop. The incident occurred on Manhattan's Upper East Side, near the junior high school where the teen was attending summer school. Powell and some other black youths had gotten into a dispute with a building superintendent right before that cop arrived on the scene.

The cop claimed that the shooting was in self-defense, that Powell came at him with a knife. Some witnesses claimed that this was not true, that Powell had his hands up when the officer fired the first shot.

Days later, on the night of Powell's funeral in Harlem, a peaceful rally turned ugly.

The unrest and rage in Harlem, which lasted six days—days of property vandalized, of stores looted, of shop windows smashed, of clashes with police—didn't stay in Harlem. It swooped across the Brooklyn Bridge and touched down in Shirley's Bed-Stuy.

The riot in Bed-Stuy broke out after a CORE mass meeting over Powell's murder. This meeting ended about 12:30 a.m. After it did, about 100 people who attended launched a protest march along Nostrand Avenue. People chanted "Killer Cops Must Go!"

Rioting started about 1:30 a.m.

In reporting on night two of this riot, the *Amsterdam News* said that people "marched into some 200 stores during a five hour rampage that blew off Fulton Street and Nostrand Avenue." At one point, about a thousand people had taken to the streets.

In her autobiography Shirley was mum about the rioting in Harlem, the rioting in her Bed-Stuy; she never said if she was at moments heart-sick or horrified—or scared. But she could not have been pleased. Shirley didn't believe in rioting. "What is the sense of shooting, burning, killing? What will it bring?" she'd later say to Black people who thought violence could bring about social change. "All they have to do is press a button in Washington and every Black neighborhood will be surrounded with troops and bayonets. What are you going to do against the massive forces of the government?"

So Shirley, no doubt, shook her head over the riots in New York City and over other riots in the North that summer, unrest stemming from rage and frustration over cramped roach- and rat-infested housing, failing schools, no jobs or low-paying ones, too many cops quite casual about knocking Black people upside their heads. Bleak prospects at every turn.

These were things Shirley desperately wanted to see changed—changed through new laws. And so, Shirley had kept fighting for that seat in the New York State Assembly. As she did, she had reason to continue to hope for Bed-Stuy.

In late July 1964 Mayor Robert Wagner announced a grant of $223,000 to Bed-Stuy's Youth in Action, an organization launched in 1963 by the CBCC, that coalition of groups battling for a better Bed-Stuy that Shirley had joined. Youth in Action was one of several of the city's agencies aimed at combating juvenile delinquency and helping young people from low-income families have a shot at brighter prospects. To that end, Wagner also announced a jobs program: 18,000 to 20,000 jobs in government agencies for 16- to 21-year-olds.

Shirley also had reason to hope for a better America at large. That same summer saw two major pieces of legislation in LBJ's War on Poverty.

The first was the Economic Opportunity Act. Among other things, it paved the way for Job Corps, a federally funded training program. This act also gave birth to VISTA (Volunteers in Service to America, later renamed AmeriCorps VISTA). VISTA created job opportunities (tutoring, for example) in urban and rural communities around the country.

The second major piece of legislation was the Food Stamp Act. It created a permanent national program that helped people from low-income households buy groceries and other essential goods. The program was later named the Supplemental Nutrition Assistance Program, or SNAP.

LBJ wanted to do more if elected president in November, more to combat poverty, more toward the building of the Great Society. But after the riots he was worried. He feared a white backlash—feared that white people who were for Jim Crow and even some whites who had supported things such as the Civil Rights Act might point to the riots as proof that Black people weren't worthy of full citizenship, of equality of opportunity, and so turn against him.

LBJ's Republican opponent was Arizona's Senator Barry Goldwater, who blamed Black leaders for the riots. The people he pointed the finger at included James Farmer, co-founder of CORE and an architect of the Freedom Rides back in 1961. Goldwater charged that people like Farmer and their white allies—people crusading for equality of opportunity, for justice—promoted lawlessness and disrespect for authority.

Goldwater put himself out there as a law-and-order man and called for limited government spending. If elected, he would halt the construction of the Great Society and put an end to the War on Poverty.

★ ★ ★

As election day neared, around the nation the central question was, would voters say yes or no to the Great Society? Yes or no to LBJ?

Yes or no?

But at least in Brooklyn, the 17th AD was poised to say yes to Shirley Chisholm.

CHAPTER 9

PASO A PASO

ON TUESDAY, NOVEMBER 3, 1964, THE UNITED STATES
said yes to the Great Society.

LBJ won in one of the largest landslides in U.S. history. He won 44 states and the District of Columbia.

When Shirley became Brooklyn's first Black woman elected to the New York State Assembly, hers was a spectacular victory. To Simeon Golar's 922 votes and the Reverend Charles Lewis's 1,893 votes, Shirley got a whopping 18,151 votes. Ironically, one of the prominent white politicians who had backed her was Stan Steingut, who at one point in the 1950s represented the 17th AD and who years earlier, at Brooklyn College, had insisted that Black people didn't have the right stuff for leadership.

★ ★ ★

In "The Lady Is Also a First," *Amsterdam News* columnist Daphne Sheppard gave her readers a snapshot of Shirley on election night.

Sheppard wrote of Shirley sporting "her feathered Robin Hood cap perched at a jaunty angle and trailing a beige-lined scarlet cape from her irrepressible shoulders." She also reported that Shirley "spouted Spanish and English felicitations to the milling and cheering constituents."

Shirley's fluency in Spanish had been a definite plus during the campaign. On the night of her victory, she gave Puerto Ricans in the crowd a big thank you!

"*Paso a paso se va lejos,*" she said at one point—"Step by step one goes far."

Shirley's victory was bittersweet, however. There was one precious vote that she did not get. Her first cheerleader, the person who told her that she would be a great woman, who said, "I know you have it, Shirls"— Papa, who had become a naturalized citizen in the 1940s and thus eligible to vote, had died the year before.

Charles Christopher St. Hill, who suffered from high blood pressure, had been gardening on the grounds of his prized home on Prospect Place when a devil of a headache hit. Once inside that home, he took a seat, then died.

Shirley was at work when she got the telephone call. "I collapsed screaming and had to be given a sedative."

"I almost went to pieces," she told a reporter years later.

"Almost" being the important word. She had stayed in the political fray while still in mourning, then had gone on to campaign for that assembly seat.

"My election would have made him so proud," she later wrote, "it was even more than he had hoped for me."

★ ★ ★

After Shirley won that assembly seat that would have made Papa so proud, she got some much needed rest. She and Conrad took a trip to Jamaica. In mid-December Daphne Sheppard reported that Assembly-woman-elect Shirley Chisholm was "making white sand castles on Montego Bay."

When the Chisholms got back from vacation, Shirley was fired up to build things far more substantive than sandcastles, things not easily washed away by ocean waves.

CHAPTER 10

THE PEPPERPOT

"AT FIRST GLANCE, IT LOOKS LIKE IT COULD BE A
victorian estate, a humongous hotel with plenty of sleeping quarters,
or a stunning Gothic castle with a gazillion windows and stairways one
might find in another country."

This was travel writer and photographer Theresa St. John talking
about the New York State Capitol perched upon a hill on downtown
Albany's State Street.

The Empire State's magnificent capitol building was, said another
writer, "a testament to the state's architectural might and the moxie of
New Yorkers and their government."

In this colossal magnificence, on January 6, 1965, pint-size Shirley
Anita St. Hill Chisholm, herself so full of might and moxie, took the oath
of office as a member of the 175th New York State Legislature.

About 60 percent of the 208 members of this legislature—150 in the
assembly, 58 in the senate—were lawyers. The rest were a mixed lot—
from farmers, teachers, and two radio station operators, to a funeral
director, a casket maker, and a landscaper. There was a tentmaker too.

Shirley was one of only four women in the assembly. The other three
were white.

Shirley was one of only six Black assembly members. The other five
were men. They included former Tuskegee Airman and Freedom Rider
Percy Sutton, representing a district in Harlem; the old political hand Bert
Baker, representing Brooklyn's sixth district; and Buffalo businessman

Arthur Hardwick, Jr., representing a district in Erie County. And Hardwick was someone with whom Shirley would one day have a very serious relationship.

★ ★ ★

Before Shirley and others in the assembly could get down to the business of going to bat for the people in their districts, there was a battle over who would serve as the assembly's speaker, or presiding officer.

More than 40 years later, New York City's first Black mayor, David Dinkins, who joined the assembly in 1966, remembered that back then "the Speaker had even more authority than he has today—no legislation saw the light of day if the Speaker said no, and he appointed the chairs of all committees and hired and fired all assembly employees. His power was enormous."

Democrats outnumbered Republicans 88-62 in the assembly, so the speaker was going to be a Democrat. The contest was between two Brooklynites: Stan Steingut from the 18th AD and Anthony "Tony" Travia from the 22nd AD.

The people's business was on hold for two long months during which time there were endless huddles, arm twisting, tests of loyalty.

"No one was paying any attention to me," Shirley later wrote. "I was a woman and a newcomer."

Steingut's camp just assumed that she'd vote for Steingut. Not just because he had backed her run for the assembly. She was still tight with Tom Jones, who was tight with Steingut.

Folks were shocked when they learned that Shirley was going to vote for Travia. One politician told her that she'd be committing "political suicide" if she didn't vote for Steingut.

Shirley was not about to go along to get along, not about to be bossed around. She didn't really know Travia, but she had heard terrific things about his service when he was the Democratic leader in the assembly for the eight long years that it was in Republican control. Why kick him to the curb now?

And he wasn't. Tony Travia got the speakership.

★ ★ ★

Being a member of the state assembly or senate isn't a full-time, year-round job. The legislature is usually only in session from early January until June. And during those months, not every day of the week. So it made no sense for Shirley and Conrad to move upstate. With some 150 miles between Albany and Brooklyn, it also made no sense for Shirley to commute every day.

The Chisholms had a new rhythm to their lives. Shirley lived in Brooklyn some days and in Albany other days. At the time the Chisholm home was at 715 St. Marks Avenue.

★ ★ ★

In Albany Shirley bunked across the street from the capitol building at the DeWitt Clinton Hotel, something of a Democratic clubhouse. It was where politicians cut deals in rooms, suites, and in the Shelf, the hotel's bar.

Shirley made no mention in her autobiography of socializing with the other women in the assembly. Some men, she said, "made persistent and sometimes ingenious efforts" to get her to join them in a little nightlife. Shirley, who still loved to dance, declined. She wasn't in Albany to have a good time, but to work, work, *work*.

Holed up in her hotel room, where she took most of her meals, if not watching a little TV, Shirley pored over legislation, prepped for debates.

No doubt it was in that hotel room and perhaps during her commutes that Shirley thought about and drafted legislation to improve the lives of the people in her district and others in the Empire State. For their sakes she sponsored and co-sponsored bill after bill after bill.

For day care centers for the children of single mothers and for other families who really needed them.

For would-be police officers to complete courses in "civil rights, civil liberties, minority problems and race relations."

For unemployment insurance for domestic workers in private homes. "Every black woman in New York City, including my own mother," she told her colleagues, "has done cleaning work at some time. But whenever they were out of work they got nothing."

Shirley fought for New York to do better by its people—build a better society.

And she didn't hold her tongue when she got pushback, as happened in spring 1965 when she championed a bill for public schools to teach "human relations" in U.S. history, what would later be called multicultural studies.

Assemblywoman Constance Cook called the bill "a dangerous step."

"It is a bill to make us aware that all people of all races have a contribution," Shirley countered.

For the stands she took and for the way she spoke up, spoke out, Shirley was dubbed "the pepperpot."

Meaning?

"That's because I breathe fire," she told a journalist.

Assemblywoman Pepperpot was on fire for boards of education throughout New York State to provide pre-K for children in poor neighborhoods.

For would-be teachers to pass at least one course in race relations or Black history.

For high school graduation requirements to include passing courses on the dangers of alcohol and drug abuse.

For money to renovate—including fireproofing—and better maintain the Brooklyn Children's Museum near Bed-Stuy in Crown Heights.

Between early 1965 and the summer of 1968, Assemblywoman Shirley Chisholm introduced more than 90 bills and co-sponsored 51. As has always been the case, of the thousands of bills put forward in a state legislature, only a handful ever pass and are signed into law by a governor. So it's not surprising that only a handful of Shirley's bills became law. It's equally true that Shirley's bills that became law had a profound impact on New York State and would continue to do so far into the future.

They included the one for unemployment insurance for domestic workers in private homes, one for raising the maximum amount of money a public school could spend per pupil from $500 to $600, and one that ended what Shirley called "outrageous legal discrimination" against women teachers. If a teacher chose to have a baby and took maternity leave, when she returned to work she lost her tenure rights—that is, she'd be treated like a newbie and could easily be fired. "My bill changed that," Shirley proudly wrote.

The assembly bill she is best known for is the one that created the Search for Education, Elevation and Knowledge program, better known as SEEK. The program's goal was to level the playing field when it came to college. It allowed young people who had received a subpar education and so were not quite college-ready to be admitted to the City University of New York (CUNY) colleges, where they'd take special classes to bring them up to speed in, say, English composition.

In preparing for the SEEK legislation, Shirley had visited 26 Brooklyn schools incognito. Some in Black neighborhoods, some in white ones.

And this was at a time when most New York City public school teachers, principals, and other administrators were white.

Four things stood out when it came to the schools in Black neighborhoods: the large number of substitute teachers; the absence of a rigorous curriculum; teachers with low expectations of Black girls and boys; and the lack of say for many Black parents in the Parent-Teacher Association. SEEK gave students in such schools a fighting chance to rise in life.

But SEEK might never have become a reality had it not been for the "Midnight March."

— ★ ★ ★ —

The Midnight March happened in 1966. Led by Shirley and Percy Sutton, Black lawmakers visited Speaker Travia's room in the DeWitt Clinton. "We were sitting on the floor, on the radiator, on the side of a bed—all crowded in to Tony's small hotel room," remembered David Dinkins.

It was a bold move. As Dinkins explained, "it was unheard of for black legislators to go to the mighty Speaker and bargain for their constituents and themselves."

But bargain they did. In exchange for their support of Travia for speaker in the next election, they wanted his support for the SEEK bill.

— ★ ★ ★ —

When Assemblywoman Shirley Chisholm was back in Brooklyn, she was out and about among the people a lot.

Attending the kickoff of a fundraiser for Bed-Stuy's Boys' Club.

Speaking at an annual Salute to Finer Womanhood Luncheon.

Being celebrated by some 300 people at a dinner held at Concord Baptist Church.

Cheering on the Hancock Neighborhood Council's cleanup drive of a five-block area.

No matter how much she did up in Albany and in her community, for some folks it was never enough.

"During the last election of Nov. 1964, you mentioned Mrs. Shirley Chisholm's name quite often and with much enthusiasm," wrote a Brooklynite to the *Amsterdam News*'s Daphne Sheppard in the summer of 1965. The writer, who signed the letter "A Reader from Brooklyn," claimed to have voted for Shirley but was now very disappointed in her. That's because A Reader from Brooklyn passed, daily, the senior citizen home on St. Johns Place and was horrified to see it in such terrible shape.

Its fence was broken.

Its yard needed some serious TLC.

"I'm sure Mrs. Chisholm also passes this way," the reader continued, "but with her new position, has she become blind?" This person hoped not only that the newspaper would publish the letter but also that Shirley would read it and remember "that without certain support" she would not have become an assemblywoman.

Shirley read that letter all right.

"The fact that I am now the Assemblywoman in no way means that I or anyone else elected to public office can cure the many ills and wrongs that beset our community," she replied.

Blind to the needs of her community?

"I [have] been able to pass and have signed into law by the Governor seven bills I sponsored and fought for to benefit the people in this community." Shirley repeated the fact that no one person can solve a community's every problem. She then advised A Reader from Brooklyn to write to the president of the home's board of directors.

While Shirley worked in the assembly, attended events in her community, was celebrated (and occasionally scolded), she had her sights set on playing a role in the governance of the nation.

It was something she shared with Dinkins in 1966—something he thought delusional.

"David, I'm going to be the first black woman in Congress."

Two years later, she was hard at work to make that dream a reality.

CHAPTER 11

FIGHTING SHIRLEY CHISHOLM

IT TOOK GUTS TO DREAM OF BECOMING THE FIRST black woman in the U.S. Congress.

It took even more guts to speak that dream.

In 1916 women's rights activist Jeannette Rankin, a white Republican from Montana, became the first woman elected to the U.S. House of Representatives. This was four years before American women won the right to vote nationwide through the 19th Amendment. And that was something for which Rankin had fought mightily.

By 1968 the number of women who had served in the House since Rankin was tiny: 240, making up less than 4 percent of the House during those years. Of that number, only Hawaii's Patsy Mink, a Japanese American Democrat, first elected in 1964, was a woman of color. When it came to the U.S. Senate, by 1968 only 10 women, all white, had served in that branch of Congress.

There had never been a whole lot of Black men in the House. Fourteen served in the House during Reconstruction, when the nation was putting itself back together following the Civil War.

With the rise of Jim Crow and the white backlash against racial justice, the number of Black men in the House dropped. In the 1880s, 1890s, and early 1900s, there were seven.

Then none.

Until 1929, when Oscar Stanton De Priest from the South Side of Chicago was elected. After him, only a handful of other Black men, among them Harlem's Adam Clayton Powell, Jr., were elected to the House by 1968. As for the Senate, in the 1870s and 1880s—just two. There wasn't another one until the election of Ed Brooke of Massachusetts in 1966.

Shirley didn't let the numbers stop her.

★ ★ ★

The congressional district Shirley wanted to represent was the newly redrawn 12th, which included Bed-Stuy. The redrawn 12th was thanks to the valiant effort of Shirley's former Unity Democratic Club colleague Andy Cooper.

In 1966 Cooper was the lead plaintiff in a lawsuit that sought to remedy what he called the "tortuous, artificial and labyrinthine" way congressional districts in Brooklyn had been created, mostly as it impacted Bed-Stuy. The neighborhood, still predominantly Black, had been unfairly divided up, or gerrymandered, by white politicians in a way that split it between five congressional districts, all represented by white people.

The lawsuit cost Andy and Jocelyn Cooper a lot of money, but their sacrifices paid off. Cooper's lawsuit led to a similar lawsuit by other parties, and in December 1967 the U.S. Supreme Court ruled that the way that Bed-Stuy was split up was unconstitutional. It went against the Voting Rights Act of 1965. Signed into law by President Johnson back in August 1965, this major piece of legislation was created chiefly to end the widespread suppression of the Black vote in the South.

When the map for the 12th Congressional District (CD) was redrawn, it would be 70 percent Black. In addition to Bed-Stuy, it would include parts of largely Italian Bushwick, largely Jewish Crown Heights, mostly Puerto Rican and Jewish Williamsburg, and Greenpoint with its large Polish community.

Back when Cooper sought Assemblywoman Chisholm's support in his lawsuit, he was met with silence. Shirley apparently didn't see it in her best interest to support Cooper in a lawsuit—one opposed by Stan Steingut and other Brooklyn Democratic bosses. Shirley, it seems, didn't want to get on the wrong side of them. But after Cooper succeeded and the new 12th CD was a reality in 1968, Shirley was all over it.

Actually, she was all over it before the final district lines were made public in early 1968. Back in December 1967, a few days after Christmas, a group of Brooklynites picked Shirley as their candidate for the new congressional seat.

"Mrs. Shirley Chisholm has already established a reputation for political independence," announced this organization, the Committee for a Negro Congressman from Brooklyn. It was made up of Black people, white people, and Puerto Ricans.

When, shortly before midnight on Thursday, December 28, Shirley got the call that she had been chosen—

"I was excited, somewhat overwhelmed and very ecstatic," she told the *Amsterdam News*. "I realized very quickly that ever since I had entered the political arena, the Bedford-Stuyvesant community has made me a winner. I, now, suddenly realize that the greatest fight in my life is about to take place, and once again the people in this community will determine my political destiny on the basis of my record, my independence and courage."

★ ★ ★

In the Democratic primary Shirley would face two Black candidates. One was Brooklyn's first Black state senator, Willie Thompson, a

Brooklyn College alum like Shirley and also of Bajan descent. The other was a former secretary of New York State's Department of Labor, Dollie Robinson, a longtime workers' rights activist. Word was that Robinson would draw off votes from Shirley and that Thompson was a shoo-in.

Shirley got a real boost when an old friend-turned-foe turned friend again.

Mac Holder was back!

In March 1968 Holder told a reporter that after several weeks of "soul-searching," he had decided to get behind Shirley. He became her campaign manager. And he took a leave of absence from his job to do this.

While Holder worked his magic, Shirley *was* the magic. As always, alive with activity.

She tramped the streets of the 12th CD.

She reached out to folks in parks, in public housing, on street corners, in churches, and at probably more house parties than she could count—parties hosted by women.

"In the black neighborhood I ate chitlins, in the Jewish neighborhood bagels and lox, in the Puerto Rican neighborhood arroz con pollo."

When pounding the pavement or when in a vehicle equipped with a loudspeaker on top and a microphone inside (a sound truck), she often introduced herself as "Fighting Shirley Chisholm."

"Sock it to 'em, Shirley!" folks often shouted back.

Once again, Shirley knew she had to reach women, women, *women!* Once again, she knew the math: There were somewhere between 10,000 and 13,000 more registered women voters than men voters in the 12th CD.

Just as when she ran for the assembly, a whole lot of women had Shirley's back. Conrad once said that his wife could telephone 200 women out of the blue and they'd be at the Chisholm home in an hour. Ready to fight for Shirley.

Make phone calls.

Ring doorbells.

Tramp the streets with shopping bags bulging with campaign literature to hand out, likely in parks and playgrounds, in barbershops and beauty parlors, in diners and cafés, on subway platforms, at bus stops—women, women, *women* spreading the word about her campaign.

And her slogan: "Fighting Shirley Chisholm—Unbought and Unbossed!"

Unbought?

She was an independent politician beholden only to the people.

Unbossed?

She was not going to be bullied or pushed around.

★ ★ ★

While troops of women, especially Black women of Bed-Stuy, worked *hard* on her campaign, Assemblywoman Chisholm was still hard at work for the people. For example, in March 1968, with other New York lawmakers, she signed a letter to Governor Nelson Rockefeller in protest of a bill he had recently signed that cut some $300 million a year from Medicaid, the state's health-care program for low-income people. The cut was $100 million *more* than the governor had originally announced.

In that letter Shirley and company also took Rockefeller to task for expanding the shoot-to-kill law. Now cops could use deadly force against a fleeing suspect so long as they *thought* the person was armed.

The amped-up shoot-to-kill law was in reaction to the "Long

Hot Summer of 1967": Black rioting in Chicago, Cincinnati, Detroit, Milwaukee, Newark, and in scores of other cities. As in the past, these riots were explosions of anger and resentment over police brutality and a system that kept so many locked out of quality education, decent housing, good jobs, a system that kept so many locked into poverty and bleak futures. That long hot summer had included riots in Harlem and in Bed-Stuy.

More unrest came in 1968 following the assassination of Martin Luther King, Jr., on April 4 in Memphis, Tennessee, where he was giving his support to Black sanitation workers on strike for decent wages and working conditions.

Baltimore. Chicago. Detroit. Kansas City. Washington, D.C. Uprisings erupted all over the nation in the wake of King's murder. There might have been one in Indianapolis had it not been for New York U.S. senator Bobby Kennedy, JFK's younger brother. That spring, Kennedy, who had walked the streets of Bed-Stuy, someone deeply aggrieved by poverty and racism in the United States, was seeking to be the Democratic candidate for president.

On the day that King was killed, Kennedy was scheduled to give a campaign speech in the heart of Black Indianapolis, 17th and Broadway. When he arrived on the scene, the crowd of some 2,500 people only knew that King had been shot. It was from Kennedy that they learned that King was, in fact, dead.

Kennedy called for calm, for peace, for people to replace any rising hate and rage with compassion and love. He asked the crowd to pray for King's family, to pray for the nation. Weeks later, people would have Kennedy's family in their prayers.

On June 5, shortly after midnight, at L.A.'s Ambassador Hotel where Kennedy was celebrating a victory in the California primary, a lone gunman shot him once in the head, twice in the back. Kennedy died the next day.

Two public figures calling for social justice were killed within two months. Shirley later called "the loss" of King and Kennedy "an incalculable one, but if the effect was to frighten any potentially controversial figure into seclusion and inactivity, the damage would be greater still." In other words, people fighting for social justice needed to not be intimidated into withdrawing from that fight.

On Shirley campaigned to be a public figure on the national stage.

Paso a paso. First she had to win the New York primary on June 18.

★ ★ ★

On June 19, 1968, at 1:30 a.m. word reached Shirley at her campaign headquarters on Bergen Street that, yes, she had done it again. It was close: With 5,431 votes, Shirley beat Robinson by 3,680 votes, and she beat Thompson by only 788 votes.

But a win is a win.

At her headquarters, Shirley was decked out in a lavender floral dress with handbag and shoes to match when she heartily thanked her supporters. She told them that from the start of her campaign, she was "aware of the barriers, hidden and otherwise," in her path. But she had carried on her run for Congress because of "the faith that the people of Bedford-Stuyvesant had" in her: "It was the people who insisted that I remain in the fight because they desired a voice that belongs to them; they desired a representative with integrity and sincerity."

She ended on a most confident note: "Thus, I look forward to victory in November, as the first black woman to go to Congress with the help of the people."

CHAPTER 12

★ ★ ★ ★ ★ ★ ★ ★ ★

TOUGH, BABY

IN THE GENERAL ELECTION SHIRLEY FACED TWO MEN.

One was the Conservative Party's Ralph Carrano of Greenpoint, a white cab driver. Shirley couldn't have been worried about him because the 12th Congressional District didn't have a lot of conservatives.

The other candidate, however, was most definitely someone to worry about. He was James Farmer, a big shot—one of the most prominent civil rights leaders of the day. Farmer was physically a giant of a man with a bass-baritone voice that could truly boom.

Running on the ticket of both the Republican and Liberal parties, Farmer had the backing of New York City's Mayor John Lindsay, Governor Nelson Rockefeller, and a bunch of other major politicians in New York and around the nation. The *New Pittsburgh Courier* reported on this back in early June 1968. The headline: "Farmer's Chances Are Good."

Shirley's health was anything but. She had a tumor in her pelvis— and it had to be removed.

In late July she went under the knife. The surgery went well, but when she left the hospital several days later, she was even skinnier.

While Shirley was recuperating, Farmer acted as if she had gotten scared or something and was about to bow out. "Where's Mrs. Chisholm?" Farmer teased.

Shirley couldn't let that stand. On a muggy August day, just three weeks after having major surgery—and with her stitches not yet out— she hurried from home with a beach towel around her waist under her clothing to disguise the weight loss. She was soon in a sound truck.

As the sound truck moved through the streets, with a microphone to her lips, the tiny but mighty pepperpot shouted out, "Ladies and gentlemen, this is Fighting Shirley Chisholm and I'm up and around in spite of what people are saying." And she was ready to keep fighting for the people.

Job creation.

Job training programs.

Better housing.

More day care centers.

These were some of her top campaign pledges.

Shirley was also concerned about the nation's escalating involvement in the Vietnam War. This involvement began back in the 1950s with the United States sending a few hundred military advisers to South Vietnam in its war against communist North Vietnam. Then in the 1960s JFK began sending combat troops.

The numbers swelled under LBJ. In 1968 alone, the war viewed as unwinnable by many Americans was costing U.S. taxpayers a whopping $77.4 billion (more than $500 billion in today's dollars). By then, there were more than a half million Americans fighting in Vietnam. Nearly 17,000 would die just that year.

As more and more Americans grew sour on the war, LBJ's prospects for another term grew dimmer and dimmer. The president became so unpopular that in March 1968 he had announced that he would not seek reelection.

Nothing was going to make Shirley quit her bid for a seat in Congress. And it was a race in which she faced heavy sexism.

Farmer argued that Black women had "been in the driver's seat" in their communities for way too long. The 12th CD needed "a man's voice in Washington," not that of a "little schoolteacher," he said. Often when campaigning in the 12th CD Farmer had an entourage of macho-looking Black men sporting big afros and beating bongo drums, symbols of the militant Black Power movement.

At the time, Black women were being blamed for what ailed poor Black families, poor Black communities. Three years earlier a Department of Labor study, *The Negro Family: The Case for National Action,* had been leaked to the press. Because this study was authored by Daniel Patrick Moynihan, then assistant secretary of the labor department, it came to be known as the Moynihan Report.

This study claimed, among other things, that Black America was plagued by too many female-headed households, that Black women were weakening Black men—that Black America was under a matriarchy, or ruled by women.

More than a few Black men bought into this and came to despise the so-called Black matriarchy, as if Black women were keeping so many Black men in low-paying jobs, as if Black women were to blame for so many Black children attending terrible schools.

Though her gender (like her size) was so often used against her, Shirley wasn't about to wage an anti-male campaign. But for those insisting that the 12th CD needed a man in Congress, she did have a ready reply: "It doesn't matter what you think, I'm going to win because I'm tough, baby."

Shirley hung tough even though Farmer's campaign had a lot more money than hers.

Shirley hung tough even though Farmer got far more coverage in the mainstream media than she did. When she complained to one TV station about this, she was basically told to get lost. "Who are you?" a man asked her, adding, "A little schoolteacher who happened to go to the Assembly."

For all his national prominence and backing from VIPs, Farmer had an Achilles' heel—a weak spot. He wasn't a Bed-Stuyer—wasn't even a Brooklynite. When he decided to run, he rented an apartment in Bed-Stuy, but really he lived in Lower Manhattan. What did he truly know about Bed-Stuy?

What's more, Mac Holder wasn't worried about the fact that Farmer appealed to bigwigs and to people who were impressed by big shots.

"I told Shirley that Farmer would appeal to the one or two percent at the top of the pyramid, the intellectuals who had read about him," Holder later recalled. "She was not to waste her time with them." He had Shirley stay grassroots, focus on winning over the everyday people—"the broad base of the pyramid."

And once again Shirley had the numbers on her side. Roughly 80 percent of the 12th CD's registered voters were Democrats, not Republicans like Farmer.

What's more, Farmer couldn't *habla español* like Shirley in a district that was 20 percent Puerto Rican.

So Shirley kept fighting, getting the backing of several small labor unions along the way.

One of the things that had inspired her early on was a visit from a woman on public assistance.

This stranger rang the Chisholms' doorbell one day and handed Shirley a crumpled envelope. Inside was a little under $10 in coins, a campaign donation from her and some of her friends.

After the woman left, Shirley burst into tears. "If I ever had any doubts, I don't now," she said to Conrad.

Farmer remained the odds-on favorite around the nation as Election Day 1968 neared. But then, just days before the election, the *Amsterdam News* reported that a major labor union, the Empire State's AFL-CIO, which had some two million members, had given Shirley the thumbs-up. "Her background, experience and record of achievement in the New York State Assembly has earned her the union's support," said Raymond R. Corbett, the union's president.

And on November 6, 1968, the day after the election, Shirley was in the news big time.

In Anniston, Alabama's *Anniston Star:* "Brooklyn Elects First Negro Congresswoman."

In Wisconsin Rapids's *Daily Tribune:* "First Negro Woman Wins Congressional Seat."

In the *New York Times:* "Mrs. Chisholm Defeats Farmer, Is First Negro Woman in House."

The "little schoolteacher" had gotten more than 66 percent of the vote: 34,885 votes to Farmer's 13,777 and Carrano's 3,771.

"My dear friends, tonight is a very important night, not so much for me, but for you, the people of this community," Shirley said to her supporters on election night. "After many years of struggle and sacrifices on the part of several of you here this evening, we have at long last been able to elect today a voice that shall be your voice in the halls of the United States Congress."

Shirley's victory occurred in a year that reporter Judy Klemesrud would say "may well go down in history as the Year of the Woman."

Why?

Women in Mississippi gained the right to serve on juries in 1968.

The Equal Employment Opportunity Commission ruled that flight attendants—all women back then and called stewardesses—couldn't be forced to retire if they married or when they turned 32.

Princeton and Yale Universities were poised to admit women.

In November 1968 model Naomi Sims became the first Black woman to appear on the cover of a major white-owned women's magazine, *Ladies Home Journal.*

Klemesrud also cited as "another major 'first' " Shirley becoming the first Black woman elected to Congress.

She'd be joining a handful of Black men in the House. They included Adam Clayton Powell, Jr., in his 12th term.

★ ★ ★

Back on the morning after Election Day 1968, starting at about 6 a.m., Shirley's telephone was ringing off the hook. Folks were ringing her doorbell too.

And there was Shirley with but two hours of sleep.

"Friends, relatives, well-wishers, network television crews and reporters and photographers from magazines streamed through" Shirley and Conrad's home until about six that evening, reported the *Oakland Tribune*'s Dolores Alexander. Remarkably, at the end of the day, Shirley, in a pink paisley print silk dress, "still retained her freshness."

And Shirley couldn't wait to get to D.C. and start using, on behalf of her constituents, what she saw as her most powerful political asset.

"My mouth," she told journalist Beatrice Berg in December 1968.

When interviewed by Berg, Shirley was thinking about where she would live in D.C. when Congress was in session. Her plan was to head to D.C. on Sunday evenings and return Thursday evenings. By then, home for the Chisholms was what Berg called a "cheerful duplex." It was in a brownstone at 1165 Sterling Place.

★ ★ ★

On Christmas 1968, more than a thousand people turned out at Brooklyn's Hotel St. George for a grand victory dinner for

Congresswoman-elect Shirley Chisholm. The affair, which went past midnight, began with cocktails at 6:30 p.m. in the hotel's grand salon. That was followed by dinner in the grand ballroom.

Daphne Sheppard reported that the cover of the souvenir program portrayed Shirley as "a torchbearer" following in the footsteps of four legendary women: poet Phillis Wheatley; 19th-century abolitionist, feminist, and preacher Sojourner Truth; Underground Railroad conductor and Civil War Union spy Harriet Tubman; and educator and stateswoman Mary McLeod Bethune. In the 1930s Bethune had founded the National Council of Negro Women, which would become the largest women's civil rights organization.

Shirley's supporters who couldn't afford to dine at the posh Hotel St. George got a chance to salute her too. A few days before that tribute at the St. George, the *Amsterdam News* reported on an upcoming afternoon reception at Concord Baptist Church for Shirley and other recently elected Bed-Stuy public officials. It was a free event sponsored by Bed-Stuy's Youth in Action.

Explained event co-chairs Joyce Coppin and John Ward: "Many of the voting residents in our area have not been able to greet their elected officials since the election, nor have they been privileged to attend any of the receptions given in their honor because of finance and other limitations and consequently feel 'left out.' "

The item was headlined: "Poor to Honor Shirley."

★ ★ ★ ★ ★ ★ ★ ★ ★

CHAPTER 13

DOING HER THING

ON JANUARY 3, 1969, SHIRLEY ANITA ST. HILL CHISHOLM

was sworn in as the United States' first "black woman congressman," as she liked to be called.

And out of the gate Madam Pepperpot was shaking things up.

When asked her preference for a committee assignment, Shirley's first choice was the Committee on Education and Labor. It was concerned with students, along with workers, being able to succeed in an ever changing economy.

Second choice: the Committee on Banking and Currency. Among other things, it controlled funds for housing construction. Alongside jobs and better schools, better housing was a pressing need for many low-income people Shirley well knew.

She would've also been happy to serve on the Post Office and Civil Service Committee because a lot of Black people were postal workers.

The Government Operations Committee would have been fine too. That would allow her, she said, to satisfy her "curiosity about how government decisions are made and how federal money is spent."

But the question about her committee preferences was just a formality. Her wishes carried no weight. The Democratic Committee on Committees assigned her to Agriculture.

Agriculture?

For someone representing an absolutely, positively urban district?

On second thought, perhaps that wasn't such a bum assignment. Agriculture, Shirley quickly realized, controlled the food stamp and surplus food programs, blessings for the poor.

But then Shirley learned the subcommittee to which she had been assigned: Rural Development and Forestry.

First-year congresspeople might react to committee assignments with a gulp or silent groan, but rarely with protest.

Not Shirley.

She bypassed the head of Democratic committee appointments. She appealed directly to the speaker of the House, John McCormack. She asked to be assigned to a committee more relevant to her district.

Speaker McCormack heard her out but in the end said, "Mrs. Chisholm, this is the way it is. You have to be a good soldier."

"It does not make sense to put a black woman representative on a subcommittee dealing with forestry," Shirley replied. She then added, "If you do not assist me, I will have to do my own thing."

"Your what?"

Mr. Speaker wasn't fluent in slang.

"It means I will do what I have to do, regardless of the consequences," she explained. "Doing your thing means that if you have strong feelings about something, you do it."

On January 29, the Associated Press reported on what Shirley did. "A first-term congresswoman, in an almost unprecedented move, today upset a House leadership decision that had given her an unwanted committee assignment." Shirley had "made a ringing plea to her colleagues to kill the assignment."

Doing her thing paid off. Shirley was reassigned to the Committee on Veterans' Affairs. She could live with that. "There are a lot more veterans in my district than there are trees," she told people.

During this drama Shirley was putting on a brave face in public while dealing with some serious slights and a major scare.

There was a group of congressmen from the South who balked against her sitting with them in the House dining room.

There was the Southerner who spat into his handkerchief whenever she passed his seat in the House chamber.

One Sunday night, when she returned from Brooklyn to her studio apartment in D.C.'s Capitol Park complex, she found her front door jimmied, her apartment ransacked.

Gone was her best mink-trimmed coat.

Gone were the finest four of nine knit suits.

This was within days of her swearing in.

Shirley vowed to be more vigilant. "I don't want anybody to know where I live," she told a reporter. "I don't want anybody visiting my home. All my mail, personal and otherwise, will come to my office. That's my address from here on in." By then, she had moved.

As for her person, Shirley was confident that she could protect herself. "You have to have more than a fast tongue if you are a woman." Whether the pepperpot was prepared to protect herself with pepper spray or with something more lethal, she didn't say.

Though she granted the interview about the robbery, Shirley was ambivalent about the attention. "I don't like this kind of publicity," she said. "I am not here to make this kind of news." No, Congresswoman Shirley Chisholm was in D.C. to make the kind of news that would improve people's lives in New York's 12th Congressional District and elsewhere in the nation.

Shirley definitely made news on March 26, when she delivered a blistering speech on the floor of the House of Representatives about why she would vote no "on every money bill that comes to the floor of this House that provides any funds for the Department of Defense. Any bill whatsoever."

She would vote no "until the time comes when our values and priorities have been turned right-side up again."

She would vote no "until the monstrous waste and shocking profits in the defense budget have been eliminated."

She would vote no until "our country starts to use its strength, its tremendous resources, for people and peace, not for profits and war."

Twelve days earlier, on March 14, newly elected President Richard Nixon announced plans for Safeguard, a new antiballistic missile system to protect U.S. missile bases. Safeguard would cost billions.

On the same day that Nixon announced plans for Safeguard, newspapers reported on upcoming budget cuts to D.C.'s Head Start summer program for children in low-income families.

"As a teacher, and as a woman," Shirley said two weeks later in her anti-defense spending speech, "I do not think I will ever understand what kind of values can be involved in spending $9 billion—and more, I am sure—on elaborate, unnecessary, and impractical weapons when several thousand disadvantaged children in the nation's capital get nothing."

In this, her first speech in the House, Shirley went off on Secretary of Defense Melvin Laird's recent calculation that U.S. forces would remain in Vietnam for at least two more years.

Two more years?

Of "hunger for Americans, of death for our best young men, of children here at home suffering the life-long handicap of not having a good education when they are young."

Two more years?

Of "high taxes, collected to feed the cancerous growth of a Defense Department budget that now consumes two-thirds of our federal income."

Two more years?

Of "too little being done to fight our greatest enemies." Those enemies, she said, were "poverty, prejudice, and neglect" in America.

Shirley was one of 16 members of the House (all Democrats) who called for the immediate withdrawal of U.S. forces from Vietnam.

★ ★ ★

When Shirley walked out of the House chamber that day, she heard one of her colleagues say to another, "You know, she's crazy!"

Other colleagues later took Shirley to task for that speech. They said that it was borderline—or outright—unpatriotic not to support defense bills when the nation was at war.

But Shirley wasn't cowed, wasn't bullied. She kept on stepping, kept doing her thing.

She did so with a growing fan base of college students. After that speech on defense spending, "student groups began to pay attention to me," she recalled. "Apparently the sharp language in my speech against the war struck a responsive chord." She was flooded with requests to speak on college campuses and she told her staff to say yes to as many as possible.

CHAPTER 14

OUTRAGEOUS

JUST AS IN THE NEW YORK STATE ASSEMBLY,

in the U.S. House of Representatives Shirley Chisholm sponsored
and co-sponsored bill after bill.

For making Martin Luther King, Jr.'s birthday a national holiday.

For senior citizens to get a cost-of-living increase in their Social
Security checks.

For more benefits for cops and firefighters disabled in the line
of duty, or for their families if they died in the line of duty.

Shirley spoke up and out for the passage of the Equal Rights
Amendment (ERA), an addition to the U.S. Constitution that would make
discrimination based on sex illegal. Drafted by white suffragists, the ERA
was first introduced in Congress more than 40 years earlier, three years
after women won the national vote.

Shirley championed the ERA on the floor of the House on May 21,
1969. "Mr. Speaker," she began, "when a young woman graduates from
college and starts looking for a job, she is likely to have a frustrating and
even demeaning experience ahead of her. If she walks into an office for an
interview, the first question she will be asked is, 'Do you type?' " With
this, Shirley was underscoring the fact that many companies saw women
as only fit to fill jobs as support staff, such as secretarial positions. While
these are important jobs, Shirley was arguing that women deserved
wider opportunities.

In fighting for the ERA, Shirley stated that she was no stranger to racial prejudice. "But the truth is that in the political world I have been far oftener discriminated against because I am a woman than because I am black." Recognizing that racism was far from dead, Shirley said that it was "becoming unacceptable," whereas sexism "is still acceptable."

Shirley also pointed out that there was no woman on the U.S. Supreme Court and no woman in the president's Cabinet—and that there'd been only two in the nation's history up to that point. What's more, at the time there were only two women ambassadors. Of the 100 U.S. senators, only one was a woman (Republican Margaret Chase Smith). Of the 435 U.S. representatives, only 10 were women.

"Considering that there are about 3½ million more women in the United States than men, this situation is outrageous," Shirley said in her hard-hitting speech.

Because of this outrageous situation, Shirley initially had an all-women staff, many of whom called her "Mrs. C."

★ ★ ★

Five days after her battle for the ERA, Mrs. C. was on the House floor fighting for the neediest Americans. With another New York lawmaker, she introduced a bill to increase federal funding for Medicaid and other public assistance—from aid to people with disabilities, to the Aid to Families with Dependent Children (AFDC) program.

Shirley, along with more than a dozen other representatives, was also fighting for the repeal of the AFDC "freeze." It was a freeze on the amount of money the federal government kicked in for the program. If a state had an increase in the number of families eligible for the AFDC after July 1, 1969, the federal government would not increase the amount of funding to match the growing need.

The AFDC freeze was repealed. But the bill on behalf of the nation's neediest that Shirley co-sponsored did not pass.

★ ★ ★

During the spring of 1969 Shirley also fought for a group of oppressed
people in Charleston, South Carolina: Black hospital workers in low-
paying jobs, including maintenance workers and kitchen staff. These
people worked at Medical College Hospital, which had zero Black
nurses and doctors.

Most of these workers, the majority of them women, were making
$1.30 an hour when the minimum wage was $1.60. After some of them
were fired for trying to meet with the hospital's president about being
underpaid, several hundred banded together to form a union, then went
on strike. They demanded that their colleagues get their jobs back and
that management recognize their union. Within days low-wage workers
at nearby Charleston County Hospital also went on strike.

It was a cause that Martin Luther King, Jr.'s widow, Coretta Scott
King, championed just as her husband had championed striking Black
sanitation workers in Memphis in 1968. Other national figures and local
folks, including Black high school students, also took to the streets in
support of the hospital workers.

Huge demonstrations led to a multitude of arrests. At one point South
Carolina's governor, Robert McNair, had members of his state's military
force, the National Guard, out patrolling the streets.

On April 29, along with 25 other members of the House, Shirley
signed a letter to President Nixon pleading with him to send his "most
trusted representative" down to Charleston to work with the hospitals
on a way forward.

The Nixon Administration pressured them to rehire those fired and
find a peaceful way for their concerns and complaints to be heard. But it

exerted no pressure on the hospitals to recognize the union, which they never did. However, after the 100-plus-day strike ended in June, the workers did get minimum wage.

★ ★ ★

On June 16, 1969, Shirley took to the House floor on behalf of young men who, for religious or political reasons, refused to serve in the armed forces after being drafted. Many people condemned them as "draft dodgers." Shirley called them "war resisters." And she didn't want to see them treated as criminals, but rather given amnesty, a pardon.

"The question of amnesty for those men who are in jail, who are in self-imposed exile, and who have deserted the military because of their conscientious opposition to the Vietnam war, has become critical," said Shirley.

Her heart ached for these young men. Roughly 700 in jail. Hundreds awaiting sentencing. Close to 5,000 had fled the country. "Untold numbers," she added, were in hiding within the nation. Along with amnesty for these young men, Shirley called for an end to the draft.

★ ★ ★

Shirley also joined the fight for a group she said was one of the most unrepresented: 18-year-olds. She was in the camp that argued if an 18-year-old could serve in the U.S. armed forces, then an 18-year-old should have the right to vote. At the time, the voting age was 21.

Shirley would keep fighting for this cause until it became a reality in 1971 through the 26th Amendment to the U.S. Constitution.

By then, Fighting Shirley Chisholm had kept busy, busy, busy!

CHAPTER 15

★ ★ ★ ★ ★ ★ ★ ★

A BETTER WAY

AS ALWAYS, THE UNITED STATES' FIRST BLACK WOMAN
congressman had energy to burn. She was alive with activity when
outside the halls of Congress.

This was at a time when the nation, too, was still so very, *very* alive
with activity.

Causes to champion.

Triumphs to celebrate.

Moments to mourn.

Mind-blowing and explosive events that left multitudes scratching
their heads, multitudes scared.

★ ★ ★

Shirley was alive with activity in D.C. in early January 1969 at a Metro-
politan Women's Democratic Club reception in her honor.

Later that month, in Brooklyn, she was heading a committee formed
to support a group of mostly Black and Puerto Rican low-wage workers at
Adelphi Hospital. They were in a showdown with management over their
right to unionize.

In mid-February Shirley was celebrated at a fancy dinner-dance at
Manhattan's Americana Hotel. There, in accepting an achievement award
from the Guardians, an association of Black police officers, Shirley
brought the crowd "to its feet four times with deafening, thunderous

applause," reported the *Amsterdam News*. Among other things, Shirley said, "No matter where I go I will never forget from whence I came." She also told the crowd, "I'm on the firing line in D.C." But she had no plans to stop doing her thing. Shirley said that with her, Congress was "dealing with one hundred pounds of dynamite."

This was during a month when college campuses were exploding with protests.

On February 5 California's governor, Ronald Reagan, declared a state of emergency at the University of California, Berkeley, where some Black students and other students of color had gone on strike. They wanted ethnic studies, better financial aid packages, and more students of color admitted to UC Berkeley. There had been rock throwing, fires, clashes with white students, with police. The California Highway Patrol came in to shore up the local cops, restore law and order.

Campus buildings seized. Vandalism. Arson. Stink bombs. At New York City's City College, at San Francisco State in California, at Wiley College in Marshall, Texas, at Eastern Michigan University in Ypsilanti. Around the nation, at predominately Black and at predominantly white colleges, Black, Puerto Rican, and other students of color wanted change and justice, from changes in curricula to the hiring of more professors of color.

Shirley, whose Harriet Tubman Society had called for Brooklyn College to offer courses in Black history in the 1940s and who had pushed for multicultural studies when she was an assemblywoman, could definitely relate, as she remained on the go.

In late March she was in Indiana addressing a crowd at Notre Dame's Community Forum on Black Power. There she said that colleges needed to "shape up" or "pay the price of campus destruction." She declared that the unrest on college campuses was a sign "of the grievous ill and decadent values of our society and our present-day leadership."

Ready to represent! Celebrating her big victory with campaign workers on Election Day 1968—the first Black woman elected to the U.S. Congress

In the New York State Capitol in March 1965 with the other assemblywomen (left to right): Democrat Dorothy Rose, Democrat Aileen Ryan, and Republican Constance Cook

Out and about among the people of Bed-Stuy a few days before Christmas 1968

"I DECIDED I WOULD HAVE TO BE A CATALYST."

THE RIGHT TO VOTE IN AN ELECTION IS THE AMERICAN WAY

LOCKED OUT BY ADELPHI HOSPITAL

Speaking up, speaking out in 1969 for beleaguered workers at Adelphi Hospital in Fort Greene, Brooklyn

Sound-trucking in Crown Heights a little over a week before she was elected to represent New York's 12th Congressional District

With staffers in her D.C. congressional office in 1970

Shirley in 1971

At a 1969 Police Athletic League block party in Williamsburg, Brooklyn

Presidential campaign button

"IF THEY DON'T GIVE YOU A SEAT AT THE TABLE, BRING IN A FOLDING CHAIR."

At a press conference in the summer of 1971 with three other co-founders of the National Women's Political Caucus: Gloria Steinem (seated far left), Betty Friedan (seated far right), and Bella Abzug (standing)

On the National Mall in April 1971, addressing a crowd of mostly Vietnam veterans who marched on Washington to protest U.S. involvement in the Vietnam War

SHIRLEY CHISHOLM for PRESIDENT

"to represent all Americans"

Presidential campaign button

BRING U.S. TOGETHER

VOTE CHISHOLM 1972
UNBOUGHT AND UNBOSSED

Presidential
campaign poster

Making her historic
announcement at Concord
Baptist Church on January 25,
1972: "I stand before you today
as a candidate for the Democratic
nomination for the presidency
of the United States of America."

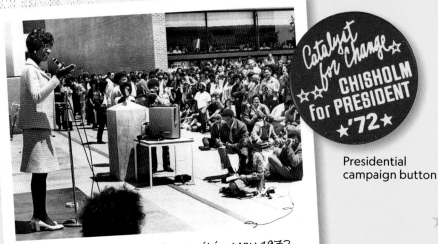

Catalyst for Change
★☆★ CHISHOLM for PRESIDENT ★'72★

Presidential campaign button

On the presidential campaign trail in May 1972 at Laney College in Oakland, California

"I'D LIKE THEM TO SAY THAT SHIRLEY CHISHOLM HAD GUTS. THAT'S HOW I'D LIKE TO BE REMEMBERED."

Defeated but ready to be a team player on July 14, 1972, after George McGovern (right of Shirley) accepted the Democratic Party's presidential nomination. Left of Shirley is Senator Hubert Humphrey.

With Coretta Scott King (middle) and Eleanor Holmes Norton (right) on March 8, 1974. Norton was just sworn in to serve a second term as head of New York City's Commission on Human Rights. In 1991 she became a congresswoman, representing D.C.

The U.S. Postal Service honored Shirley with a stamp in 2014.

Teaching at Mount Holyoke in 1984

In November 1983 with Baptist minister and civil rights activist Jesse Jackson, a Democratic party presidential hopeful for whom Shirley paved the way

A somber moment at the memorial service for Shirley in the U.S. House of Representatives on February 15, 2005, a little over a month after her passing

"YOU DON'T MAKE PROGRESS BY STANDING ON THE SIDELINES, WHIMPERING AND COMPLAINING. YOU MAKE PROGRESS BY IMPLEMENTING IDEAS."

The official congressional portrait of Fighting Shirley Chisholm. This oil painting by Kadir Nelson was unveiled in the U.S. Capitol on March 3, 2009.

In April 1969 Shirley was alive with activity at Manhattan's Hotel New Yorker. Before an audience of 150 prominent church women, she spoke about the need for "a new breed" of women and men in government, people ready to roll up their sleeves and "do all in their power to enforce existing laws for the uplift of oppressed Americans." She said that Black people would "no longer accept the bit-by-bit promises."

In May Shirley joined with Coretta Scott King and other civil rights leaders calling on people to support 2,600 of West Virginia's highway employees who had been fired after they went on strike seeking to unionize.

And Shirley stayed busy into the fall of 1969.

In September, with Adam Clayton Powell, Jr., she led the first Afro-American Day parade in Harlem. She also spoke at the Sojourner Truth Award luncheon in Rochester, New York. "In this day," said Shirley, "we are fighting for a belief in ourselves." She also spoke out about the plight of Black people, of the elderly, and of the undereducated. When she talked about how folks were rising up—Black people, students, women— she said that it boiled down to this: America needed to "wake up."

That mouth of Shirley's kept going and going in October when an estimated two million people participated in the "Moratorium to End the War in Vietnam." Some didn't go to work, others didn't go to school. There were teach-ins, rallies, marches.

Shirley was in Allentown, Pennsylvania, on that day, October 15. There she spoke to 600 high school and college students at Cedar Crest College, where classes had been canceled. The day, she said, was a "significant day in the history of our country."

Shirley later told a reporter how much she loved speaking to young people. "I talk to them about the social revolution and about reconciliation between the blacks and the whites."

In these chaotic, charged, trying times, Shirley remained alive, alive, *alive.*

Winter.

Spring.

Summer.

Fall.

"The Urban Crisis." "The Social Revolution." "Women in Politics— Why Not?" These were some of the titles of her talks.

Again and again she talked about the war in Vietnam. Again and again about the root causes of student unrest on college campuses. "While I do not condone all of their actions on the nation's campuses," Shirley told a reporter, "I do admire their determination not to accept the status quo or the decisions of their elders without question."

Back in June 1969, in her commencement address at Howard University, "Progress Through Understanding," Shirley told the graduates, "Our task at this moment in history is a great one, and if we are to perform it we must first understand what it is. We must neither withdraw from our society and nation, nor be absorbed by it. We must, for our own sakes and for everyone's sake, find a better way." Her hope, she said, was in the youth of America.

North, south, east, and west, college students were wild about Shirley. Whether or not they agreed with all her ideas, she struck them as authentic, she later wrote.

The air around Shirley was alive with talk of her running for the U.S. Senate, running for New York City's mayorship.

★ ★ ★

In 1970, another year of unrest in the nation, Shirley celebrated the publication of her autobiography, *Unbought and Unbossed.* It was dedicated to Conrad—"for his deep understanding." Along with Mac Holder, Shirley counted her husband among her "closest advisers."

Charlayne Hunter reviewed *Unbought and Unbossed* for the *New York Times Book Review*. The book was not "a literary masterpiece," she wrote. But Hunter applauded "its plain talk" about what was wrong in Washington. The biggest problem, Shirley had written, was that Congress was "ruled by a small group of old men." Hunter found Shirley's book a testament to her "honesty and vigilance."

And Shirley, having won a second term in Congress in 1970, was alive with activity still.

While keeping up a busy speaking schedule, in fighting for a better America, Shirley introduced another raft of bills and resolutions in 1971.

For the president to set a date for the withdrawal of U.S. troops from Vietnam.

For a two-dollar bill in honor of 19th-century feminist Susan B. Anthony.

For a memorial to Mary McLeod Bethune in Washington, D.C.

Shirley also sought benefits for sufferers of byssinosis, a lung disease caused by prolonged exposure to the dust of cotton and other textiles like the burlap that made her dad's hands so rough and calloused.

And Shirley fought for a whole lot more—from an increase in the minimum wage and day care centers in low-income housing complexes to better treatment for prisoners, more funding for public schools, and gun control.

★ ★ ★

On behalf of America's children, Shirley joined many members of the House and Senate in saying yes to the comprehensive child development bill. It held out the promise of a network of first-rate federally funded day care centers. These day care centers would be available to people of all incomes, with people making a lot of money charged more than people of modest means. Though the bill passed both houses of Congress, Nixon would veto it.

When that bill and others she sponsored and co-sponsored went down in defeat, there were times when Shirley wanted to quit Congress. "You wonder what is the use of coming back the next day," she would soon write, given that, as she saw it, "the majority of Congress clearly" didn't "care about the children who don't have a clean, safe place to stay while their parents are at work, about the jobless men and women who have lost all hope of supporting their families except" through public assistance. The "list is endless." It saddened her, too, that "the majority of the country" didn't "care enough to throw these people out of office and replace them with representatives who would work for the victims of society instead of the victors."

Nevertheless, Shirley stayed in the fight.

★ ★ ★

It was also in 1971, in February, that, with the 12 other Black members of Congress, Shirley founded the Congressional Black Caucus. Its mission: To "promote the public welfare through legislation designed to meet the needs of millions of neglected citizens."

Months later, on July 10, Shirley co-founded the National Women's Political Caucus (NWPC) with some 300 other women. They included Dorothy Height, president of the National Council of Negro Women, and Eleanor Holmes Norton, then head of New York City's Commission on Human Rights, a first for a woman.

The NWPC's white founders included Gloria Steinem, soon to launch *Ms.* magazine; New York congresswoman Bella Abzug; and Betty Friedan, author of the best seller *The Feminine Mystique* (1963), often credited with sparking the women's liberation movement among middle-class white women. This movement, which included some middle-class Black women like Shirley and other women of color, as well as some poor and working-class women, was a campaign to end discrimination against women when it came to jobs, education—in every arena.

The NWPC was out to harness the power of American womanhood and increase the number of women in politics. Elected and appointed. Local to national.

Two weeks after the NWPC was founded, the *Amsterdam News*, noting the organization's goal, asked, "Can a Woman Be a Good President?"

The newspaper revealed the results of a survey conducted among a mixed bag of New Yorkers. One question: "Would You Like to See a Woman President of the United States?"

"I think a woman president would be fine, great and fantastic," said Dorothea Hutchinson, a filing clerk at Columbia University.

After a bit of hemming and hawing, government worker Reuben Montgomery concluded that the presidency was "too demanding for a woman."

Gail Washington, an education major at City College, thought otherwise. "We need a change of pace. We should at least see what a woman can do."

Bus driver Anthony Madiro was appalled by the idea. "Heaven forbid, no! Women are too soft-hearted. How could they make a drastic decision?" He concluded with this: "My answer is no, no, a thousand times, no!"

Sterling Clarkson, who worked for an ad agency, was a *Yes!* Men had made "such a mess out of leading this country, perhaps women could do better," he said. "They can't do any worse."

Manicurist Lisa McBride was another *No!* A woman "should devote her time to her husband, children, and home. I just don't favor women in politics."

Norma Duke, a homemaker and mother of four, gave the idea a thumbs-up. Women think "faster" than men, she said.

Rosa Brown, a librarian, said, "Of course, I'd love to see a woman president."

Rosa's first choice was Fighting Shirley Chisholm.

CHAPTER 16

CHIZM FOR PRESIDENT

LIBRARIAN ROSA BROWN WASN'T THE ONLY PERSON
who wanted to see Shirley run for president.

When Shirley spoke at colleges, students had often urged her to do just that. Time and again she responded with the line she'd tossed off years earlier to Proffy.

"I am black and I am a woman."

That didn't fly with one student. He was a young white man at a college in the South. "Well, when are we going to break this tradition?" he asked.

His question stayed with Shirley for days, weeks.

Well, when are we going to break this tradition?

So far, every U.S. president—white.

So far, every U.S. president—male.

Well, when are we going to break this tradition?

★ ★ ★

"Shirley's Hat Tentatively in Big Ring," announced the *Arizona Republic* on August 1, 1971.

"For President: A Black Woman?" asked the *Austin American-Statesman* a few days later.

"Shirley's Sticking," said New York's *Daily News* on September 15.

"A Rebel Bucks the System." That was the headline of an article in the *Philadelphia Daily News* on December 30.

In this article Shirley said that it was time for the nation to have a government made up of Black people, Native Americans, Latinos—a rainbow of Americans. And definitely women. "The whole government, the Cabinet and heads of departments should be reflective of America."

Still, Shirley hadn't said that she was definitely running for president. She had not yet made an official announcement. But she was ready to test the waters, get a feel for how much support she might get.

★ ★ ★

On January 4, 1972, Shirley began testing the waters in Florida with its sizable population of Black, Jewish, and Spanish-speaking residents.

In Miami, she gave TV and newspaper interviews. She addressed members of a conservative men's club, the Tiger Bay Club. She had a fundraising rally at Bayfront Auditorium. She delivered a speech at the University of Miami.

Shirley didn't exactly take the city by storm. The *Miami News*'s Louis Salome reported that the crowd at the university was "sparse" and that only about 175 people turned out for the fundraiser. But Salome wasn't sneering at Shirley's effort. He stated that if she ran for president and if her run had no great impact, it "will have paved the way for change later on."

As for the right then and there, Shirley didn't slow her roll. After a quick stop in West Palm Beach to give a speech—on to Tampa.

There she was scheduled to have a rap session with young people in a hotel's reception room, but no one showed up. A 1:30 p.m. press conference was a bust because many reporters had been told it would start at 4 p.m.

At the Tampa Park Plaza Shopping Center, and with a British camera crew on the scene, Shirley chowed down on barbecue chicken at the local Boss Biddy restaurant run by Black teens. But once again the turnout was pitiful.

The largest crowd Shirley drew was about 300. This was when she addressed a women's political club.

Onward to Tallahassee.

To speak at the mostly white Florida State University.

To speak at the mostly Black Florida A&M.

While in Tallahassee, she also had a press conference at the State Capitol, met Florida's governor and secretary of state, and attended a banquet.

Shirley's time in Florida also included a quick stop in Pensacola.

"People, people, people," she chanted at a rally there, in, said a reporter, "her never faltering machine-gun bursts of speech." Continued Shirley: "I am the people's candidate and I must see to the people."

"Television lights were ice-white," said the reporter, "but Shirley Chisholm didn't blink, her glance during questions equally piercing."

In Pensacola, Shirley also teased some big news. She told supporters to be on the lookout for "an important political announcement" on January 25 in New York City.

Last stop: Jacksonville.

A youth rally at Edward Waters College, where about 2,000 people showed up.

A reception.

A chat with a TV reporter.

A banquet.

There was also a breakfast hosted by two major women's organizations to which she belonged. One was the League of Women Voters, established in 1920 to increase women's political awareness and engagement. The other was the much younger National Organization for Women (NOW). Formed in 1966, NOW's giant agenda was for women to have equality of opportunity in education, in the workplace—everywhere! (Shirley was not a founder of NOW as some sources claim.)

One thing Shirley would never forget about her time in Jacksonville was something she spotted on day one. When she stepped off the plane, she was greeted by a largely white crowd and in it was a white man with a hat that read "Chizm for President."

"You spelled my name wrong," said Shirley.

"That doesn't matter!" the man replied. "I want you for president!"

★ ★ ★

After five days in six Florida cities, Shirley jetted back to D.C. Two weeks later, she was in the elementary school auditorium of one of New York City's largest Black churches, Bed-Stuy's Concord Baptist.

With Conrad in her corner, with Mac Holder, Percy Sutton, and scores of other well-wishers rooting for her …

With TV cameras trained on her …

With a bank of microphones before her …

"I stand before you today as a candidate for the Democratic nomination for the presidency of the United States of America."

Along with expressing her pride in being a woman, her pride in being Black, along with her vow to be the candidate of the people, Shirley spoke of her faith in the American people.

"I believe that we are smart enough to correct our mistakes. I believe we are intelligent enough to recognize the talent, energy, and dedication, which all Americans, including women and minorities, have to offer."

"Give me your help at this hour!" Shirley pleaded. "Join me in an effort to reshape our society and regain control of our destiny as we go down the Chisholm Trail for 1972."

The Chisholm Trail?

Back in the 1860s a half-Cherokee, half-Scottish fur trader, merchant, and scout named Jesse Chisholm forged a famous trail that Texas ranchers used in cattle drives to railroad terminals in Kansas.

More than 100 years later, here was a Black Chisholm on a very different kind of drive.

★ ★ ★ ★ ★ ★ ★ ★ ★ ★

CHAPTER 17

TO MAKE THAT SOMEDAY COME

THE DEMOCRATIC FIELD WAS CROWDED.

The white men included Senator George McGovern of South Dakota, Senator Henry M. "Scoop" Jackson of Washington State, Senator Edmund Muskie of Maine, New York City mayor John Lindsay, and two Minnesotans, former VP (under LBJ) Hubert Humphrey and former U.S. senator Eugene McCarthy.

There was also Alabama's Governor George Wallace, the man who nearly 10 years earlier had declared "segregation now … segregation tomorrow … segregation forever."

Along with Shirley, there was one other Black person in the race for the Democratic nomination: the civil rights activist Reverend Walter Fauntroy. He was D.C.'s delegate to the House of Representatives, a representative who couldn't vote on bills but who could engage in debate and have a say on certain procedural matters.

Nor was Shirley the only woman in this race. There was also Congresswoman Patsy Mink of Hawaii.

———— ★ ★ ★ ————

Back in the summer of 1971 when Shirley began to think about running for president, she figured that she would need at least $250,000 to operate a decent campaign. She decided to take a wait-and-see approach: wait until year's end to see how many campaign contributions and pledges came in. If money flowed, she'd announce.

But Conrad and Mac Holder argued that no money would flow *until* she officially announced.

After she did on January 25, 1972, in Brooklyn, with a repeat performance a few days later in D.C., donations did come in.

Not a flood.

More like a trickle.

Nevertheless, Shirley was sticking, forging on with a campaign that was disorganized, chaotic.

Without some serious money, or "moola" as she called it, Shirley couldn't hire a professional fundraiser for all the things a campaign needs—from bumper stickers and posters to print, radio, and TV ads. Instead, supporters in this town, in that city, had to raise funds themselves for any actions they wanted to take, any events they wanted to hold on her behalf.

Without moola, Shirley couldn't hold rallies and other events in ballrooms or posh halls. This forced her to make the most of opportunities to speak at colleges and universities that didn't charge for the use of their halls and auditoriums.

Without moola, Shirley had to rely heavily on volunteers. But some weren't always reliable and others got into squabbles and power struggles.

Shirley also couldn't afford a crack public relations team to raise awareness of her campaign, get her speaking engagements along with radio and TV time, and do their utmost to see to it that when people saw or heard the name "Shirley Chisholm," it was in a positive, splendid light.

Whatever money Shirley could raise on her own went toward her travel expenses and the running of her national campaign office near Capitol Hill, in the Dodge House. There, in a small, three-room office toiled three full-time staffers, a couple of part-time staffers, and volunteers, handling everything from fielding and making phone calls to scheduling events and making reservations.

At times, Conrad manned the phones in Shirley's Brooklyn office. There, in February 1972 he told a reporter, "I encouraged her 100 percent to run for the presidency." He also sang her praises. "She's a determined person, committed and dedicated . . . Besides charisma, stick-to-it-iveness and hard work, Shirley Chisholm has qualities of leadership that people recognize and they gravitate to her. She tells it like it is. Fearless."

★ ★ ★

Some people thought that Shirley's run—with no well-oiled fundraising machine, no crack public relations team, with only a skimpy staff—wasn't so much fearless, but downright foolish.

Is she, in fact, crazy? some wondered.

Other people thought she was ego tripping.

What was really driving Shirley?

It was something that *Miami News* reporter Louis Salome recognized: That even if she went down in defeat, her run "will have paved the way for change later on."

It was something Shirley explained so beautifully and succinctly in her campaign memoir, *The Good Fight*.

She ran, she said, "to make that someday come."

A someday when no one would assume that the U.S. president had to be a white man.

A someday when people wouldn't cringe or freak out over the thought of a Black woman, or an Asian man, or a Latino man or woman, or a Jewish person in the Oval Office.

In the meantime, the White House was never the prize Shirley had her eyes on.

It was delegates: people chosen or elected to represent a state. Some pledge to a certain candidate during primary elections. Others (superdelegates) are uncommitted until the national convention. Whichever candidate has the most delegates at that convention becomes a party's nominee.

There is always a lot of bargaining at conventions. Candidates try to get other candidates to hand over their delegates in exchange for, say, a Cabinet position or other political give.

Shirley hoped to get enough delegates to influence the issues that the eventual nominee ran on, the party's platform. She wanted criminal justice reform and women's rights, for example, to be part of the Democratic Party's platform. She also wanted to see women and people of color in Cabinet positions. Other issues of importance to Shirley included better care of the environment. She would also speak out for a top-notch health-care system—for all! One that was as concerned about disease and injury prevention as it was about treating illnesses and injuries. One that took into account poisoned waterways and other environmental factors. One that made nutrition a top priority, beginning with babies in the womb.

★ ★ ★

In 1972 there were more than 20 state primary elections. No way could Shirley enter them all. For one, she didn't have the money. She had to pick and choose based on how much support she had in any given state. Shirley campaigned in none of the 11 state caucuses, which are similar to primaries, only they are run by political parties and not local and state governments.

A shoestring budget wasn't the only factor in her picking and choosing. Shirley's time was tight.

A few days here.

A weekend there.

That was usually all the time Shirley could spend in any state. She didn't want to be a no-show congresswoman, didn't want to miss out on debates about issues important to her, didn't want to miss out on voting nay on bills she abhorred and yea on ones she championed. For that, she needed to be in D.C.

★ ★ ★

When Shirley wasn't in D.C. (or Brooklyn), she was hopscotching to various states in the months after she announced her candidacy.

In the run-up to the March 14 Florida primary, Shirley was back in the Sunshine State for six days.

In the run-up to the April 25 Massachusetts primary, she spent three days in the Bay State.

In Boston she addressed a Spanish-speaking crowd in Spanish and pressed the flesh at a shopping center in its mostly Black community of Roxbury. Shirley also attended a rally at a Black church where, much to the horror of some, a group of men dressed in drag turned out—members of Boston's gay liberation movement. They were there to support Ms. Chis., as she was lovingly called throughout the campaign. These men backed Shirley because she supported their movement. She felt that their community should have the same civil rights as the straight community.

Wherever she was, whether speaking in English or in Spanish, the cornerstone of her speech was this: "The other candidates are going to be coming in here, or their campaign workers are, and saying, 'Don't vote for Shirley Chisholm, because she has no chance to be President. Vote for somebody who can win.' Well, if I can't be President, I can be an instrument for change."

This from a woman who declared herself a "shaker-upper of the system within the system!"

During her three early May days in North Carolina, the People's Candidate campaigned in one small town after the other.

She spoke to one crowd from the steps of a courthouse.

She addressed another in a muddy field.

And Shirley savored the wonderment she saw in the eyes of Black folks, people, she wrote, who were "seeing something they had never dreamed of seeing, one of their sisters running for the Presidency of the United States."

In the town of Pembroke, North Carolina, where most residents were members of the Lumbee tribe, as Shirley looked out onto the faces in the crowd, she thought about the decades of slaughter, theft, and other outrages American Indians had endured. "I broke into tears," she later wrote. "I had to fight to regain control of myself." She did manage to pull herself together and address her audience, but she didn't tell us what she said.

By then, Shirley had been out to the Midwest.

"Join with me on the Chisholm Trail!" she shouted out at a rally at Hamline University, in St. Paul, Minnesota, a city with a tiny Black population.

"If you believe in my ability, intelligence and courage, you will join me!" she cried out to an audience of about 2,000 people. "The blacks alone in America can't do it. The young people alone can't do it. The women alone can't do it. But together all these groups can rise up to get their share of the American dream and participate in the decision-making process that governs our lives."

Shirley had a terrific time at Hamline. "A program of student poetry readings and music by a black vocal group and the Hamline Jazz Lab band had warmed the audience up for a tumultuous ovation when my turn came." The applause was overwhelming. It was "one of the biggest, most enthusiastic crowds I can remember addressing." She called it "a peak moment."

Shirley had also spent two days in Michigan that began with a breakfast at a YMCA in Grand Rapids. From there she went to Kalamazoo, where before a crowd of about a thousand people in Bronson Park, she said, "We have all heard the tired rhetoric of politicians about the brotherhood of man, the American concept of democracy and equality of opportunity, and we have long noted that the politicians don't suit their actions to their words."

"Traditionally," she continued, "the Presidency has been the exclusive domain of a sole segment of our society—white males. This says to the others in our multifaceted, multiracial society that they unfortunately don't have the leadership or the brainpower to lead."

Not true, Shirley was saying. And she saw diversity as a strength!

★ ★ ★

After Kalamazoo she headed to Battle Creek, where she spoke at the dedication ceremony for a housing development.

She also made time to visit the grave of Sojourner Truth. Shirley laid a wreath there and said, "Sojourner, the battle is still going on. There are those of us who still have a commitment." She told the press that a painting of Truth hung in her D.C. office along with the words of one of Truth's most powerful speeches. "I get a great deal of strength from these things when the going gets rough."

★ ★ ★

Shirley was back in Michigan on May 15 when she got some horrifying news: One of her opponents, George Wallace, was in the hospital in critical condition. He had been shot during a campaign rally at a shopping center in Laurel, Maryland.

When Shirley heard that several Black people were under arrest, she freaked out. "If ever there was a moment when I was ready to withdraw from the campaign, this was it."

If the shooter was a Black person, Shirley thought at the time, "who knows what ugly retaliation against Blacks might follow the shooting? Who would be the prime target but me?"

She was no stranger to obscenity-laced, racist mail, no stranger to anonymous phone calls, no stranger to death threats. "It was impossible for me not to think of the risk of being attacked, a danger that had occurred to me many times before." She and Conrad had often been certain that someone was watching their home in Brooklyn.

As it turned out, no Black person had anything to do with the shooting. Wallace had been shot by a 21-year-old white man named Arthur Bremer. He had also wounded three other people in his quest to be famous. Having decided that it would be too difficult to assassinate President Nixon, Bremer trained his aim on Wallace.

Though no Black person had been involved, Shirley was still, understandably, rattled. "That unforgettable year of 1968 in which Martin Luther King's killing was followed by that of Robert F. Kennedy was still fresh in everyone's memory."

But fear didn't win. Well aware that she had a target on her back, Fighting Shirley Chisholm stayed in the race. The "risk" she decided, "had to be taken."

★ ★ ★ ★ ★ ★ ★ ★ ★

CHAPTER 18

PAVING THE WAY

MONTHS EARLIER WHEN SHIRLEY ASKED FOR

Secret Service protection, she was told no because she wasn't a major candidate. After George Wallace was shot, she got it.

And Wallace got her sympathy.

"I don't care what a person's philosophy is, I don't like to see somebody shot," Shirley told a reporter. This was shortly after the shooting, which left Wallace paralyzed from the waist down.

Later, Shirley made her actions suit her words. In early June she visited Wallace in his hospital room.

At his bedside, she wept.

He wept too.

"Is that really you, Shirley?"

"You and I don't agree," she said, "but you've been shot, and I might be shot, and we are both the children of American democracy, so I wanted to come and see you."

Shirley hadn't given the press a heads-up about the visit, but when she exited the hospital, reporters were waiting. As word spread of her visit, many people ripped into her. How in the world could she visit someone who had cried out for "segregation forever"?

"There were black politicians," Shirley recalled, "who insinuated that some kind of a deal was being cooked up!" (Wallace, by the way, would remain on the ballot.)

That wasn't the first flak Shirley got from Black politicians. From the moment she hinted that she might run, many male ones steered clear of the Chisholm Trail. They believed that if a Black person were to make a bid for the White House, that person should be a man and all Black people should throw their support behind him.

So Shirley had to put up with being belittled by some Black men, with being called "that little black matriarch." This treatment left her grateful for the wholehearted support of Percy Sutton, Congressman Parren Mitchell of Maryland, and a handful of other Black male politicians.

Shirley was also grateful for the tremendous support from a host of members of the National Organization for Women and of the National Women's Political Caucus. At the same time, she was disappointed by the lukewarm support from some key white women.

One was fellow New York congresswoman Bella Abzug, known as Battling Bella. She was on hand when Shirley officially announced in D.C. but afterward offered no rip-roaring endorsement. She told a reporter that she supported "the idea" of Shirley's run, but Bella never battled for her. Not even in New York.

Shirley had, of course, rolled on—just as she did, when, in the summer of 1972, a fake document was released that tried to ruin her.

It was a press release on stationery stolen from a Hubert Humphrey campaign office. Among other things, it claimed that in the 1950s Shirley had been in a mental institution, as a schizophrenic—this after she'd been picked up in the streets dressed like a man and menacing people. Though this press release was sent to various news outlets, apparently none of them ran with it.

But the press release got out. Shirley was devastated. She later told a reporter that many people abandoned her campaign because of it. "With tears streaming down my face, I tried to convince them that it was a fake." Many people, however, remained unconvinced. Abandoned by some followers, the slandered Shirley Chisholm kept on stepping.

It was later discovered that this press release was the handiwork of a Nixon operative. By then, the Democratic National Convention held in July 1972 in Miami Beach, Florida, had come and gone.

— ★ ★ ★ —

Ms. Chis. had ended up with 152 out of more than 3,000 delegates.

But Shirley had nothing to be ashamed about. After all, she had made it to the finish line!

In the crowded field of Democratic candidates, Patsy Mink, New York's Mayor John Lindsay, and four others had bowed out during the primaries.

Of the seven still standing at the Miami Beach Convention Center, Shirley came in fourth place behind George Wallace (with 382 delegates), Scoop Jackson (525), and the winner, George McGovern (1,729).

But what's more, the Chisholm Trail had energized thousands of young people around the country. Got them engaged in politics. Got them believing in that someday.

"Don't let the spirit die. Don't let the enthusiasm die," a very emotional Shirley told staffers and supporters when the convention was over. She told them to look on the bright side.

Lessons learned from mistakes.

Experience gained.

"I am not downhearted. I am not disillusioned. I am not bitter," she said.

But she did have one regret: "That we didn't have the moola."

— ★ ★ ★ —

On November 7, 1972, President Richard Nixon crushed McGovern.

By then, the Chisholms were dealing with crushing debt. In *The Good Fight* Shirley claimed that her campaign had spent roughly $300,000 (about $1.8 million in today's dollars). In contrast, she had raised only about $95,000.

Unpaid bills landed at the end of the Chisholm Trail—her and Conrad's doorstep. By then, home was a nine-room row house that they owned at 1028 St. Johns Place.

Despite the defeat and the debt, Ms. Chis. was committed to remaining in Congress, committed to speaking up and speaking out for the people.

CHAPTER 19

VOICE WAS NEEDED

CONGRESSWOMAN SHIRLEY CHISHOLM CONTINUED
to fight the good fight by continuing to get reelected as the voice of
New York's 12th Congressional District in Washington.

By continuing to speak up and speak out about what ailed America.

By continuing to push for the government to treat its people better.
All of its people.

In the 93rd Congress (1973-74), Shirley fought for …

Aid for services and programs related to runaway youths.

Safer schools.

More school construction.

Nutritional labeling on food.

Safer handling of food.

Handgun control.

National health care.

Prisoner rights.

Research on autism in children.

Research and education on diabetes.

For a postage stamp in honor of the first woman elected to the
U.S. Congress, Jeannette Rankin.

Shirley was also in the fight for upping the minimum wage to
$2 an hour in 1973, then to $2.20 an hour in July 1974. This was a time
when for millions of U.S. workers the minimum wage was still $1.60 an
hour. What's more, this bill had the "Chisholm provision": For the first

time in history, domestic workers were covered in the minimum wage law. When pushing for this, just as she did when in the New York State Assembly, she brought up her mom, who was still alive. "My own mother was a domestic, so I speak from personal experience when I tell you of the heavy burden household workers carry and the unfair wage that they have received."

"I have never worked so hard on a piece of legislation as I did on the Minimum Wage Bill," Shirley later told a reporter. Getting domestic workers included took, she said, "about seven months of preliminary groundwork."

She recalled telling congressmen "that the maids in their own homes didn't get enough money to provide for the basic necessities of life."

"Immediately," she also recalled, "there was a lot of flak in the cloak room." There, in the House lounge, "Congressmen began to talk about what they were paying their maids and what would happen if their maids came under the minimum wage."

For the bill to see the light of day, it needed the support of a range of groups, from women's groups and labor groups to civil rights organizations.

"I decided I would have to be a catalyst," Shirley told that reporter. "In some way I would have to try to pull these people together and talk to them from the standpoint of human dignity, pride in being a human being and wanting a decent wage to subsist on."

White southern congressmen were the toughest group, men with "preconceived attitudes about black people." What Shirley did here was invite them to come speak with her, individually, in her office. "It was so fascinating," she remembered. "Some of them didn't want me to let other Congressmen know that they were in my office." She was quite proud of the fact that "nine out of ten times, when the conversation ended," she had "won them over."

In this interview Shirley praised her staff for all their research on domestic workers' earnings in different parts of the country. And she was right proud of that research, noting that "Senator Hubert Humphrey used my research in his debate on the Senate floor. He had it read into the *Congressional Record* that he was using Mrs. Chisholm's information!"

The Chisholm provision remained in the bill, but because of pushback from President Nixon, the minimum wage only increased to $2 an hour in 1974.

★ ★ ★

While Shirley was fighting for a better, stronger, more compassionate America in Congress, while she was meeting with constituents in her Brooklyn office, while she was plenty busy with speaking engagements—

Along the way, her marriage fell apart. After nearly 30 years of marriage, she and Conrad divorced in February 1977.

When asked the month before about her marital situation, she basically told a reporter, *None of your business.* "Why is it that my private affairs are topic one in Bedford-Stuyvesant? Other Black politicians have more pressing personal problems than mine which I'm sure would make more interesting news."

Shirley wasn't single for long. She remarried before the year was out. Her new husband was Buffalo businessman Arthur Hardwick, Jr., one of the Black men who entered the New York State Assembly when she did back in 1965.

Theirs was a private ceremony held at a hotel in a suburb of Buffalo on November 26, four days before her 53rd birthday. Legally, she became Shirley Hardwick, but as a public figure she continued to be Shirley Chisholm.

Shirley never planned to be that public figure *forever,* though. She thought about quitting Congress in 1978, but people urged her to stay. "They told me that my voice was needed in the U.S. Congress." People all over the country, she said, begged her not to leave office. She changed her mind when she learned that two of the three other Black congresswomen, Barbara Jordan of Texas and Yvonne Brathwaite Burke of California, were leaving when their terms ended in 1979. "So I decided to stay in Congress and fight it out," she told a reporter. (The third Black congresswoman was Chicago's Cardiss Collins.)

But then, a few years later, on February 11, 1982, Fighting Shirley Chisholm announced that she would not seek an eighth term.

Of the 11 female Democrats in the House, she had been there the longest. What's more, having gone from the Committee on Veterans' Affairs to the Committee on Education and Labor, since 1977 she was a member of the powerful Rules Committee. It has the say over which bills are considered for a debate or a vote and which get ignored. Shirley was the second woman and the first Black woman to have a seat at that table.

By the time she announced that she was leaving Congress, Shirley had vigorously supported and helped pass Title IX, an amendment to a law on education that bans sex discrimination in educational programs and activities (such as college sports) that get federal assistance. She had co-founded the Congressional Women's Caucus devoted to furthering women's issues. She had battled to save the Office of Economic Opportunity, the agency that administered War on Poverty programs such as Head Start. She had been very instrumental in expanding the food stamp program and the federal school lunch program. She had also played a key role in the creation of the program Women, Infants, and Children, better known as WIC. Originally created to provide extra, healthy food to low-income pregnant women, new mothers, their babies, and their very young children, WIC eventually grew to include other services, such as guidance on healthy diets and referrals to health care.

Shirley had also been behind a bill that provided more money for remedial educational programs in Black and brown communities with terrible schools. "I have seen the results," she told a reporter in 1980. Those results included the discovery of gifted children in communities that many people had written off. "A child in a ghetto school with no science laboratories" and other extra materials was, she said, "a child that frequently becomes educationally dead."

In 1982 there was still so much to fight for, legislation that would improve the lives of people in her district and around the nation, but Shirley stood firm in her decision to leave Congress.

She had come to dread going back to her district on weekends, a district that still had a lot of people living in or on the brink of poverty.

"Every time I go back, more and more people have lost their jobs, more and more people have had to give up their homes because they couldn't pay the mortgage," Shirley told the *Philadelphia Inquirer*'s Kathy Hacker.

And every time the congresswoman went back to her district, more and more people were fighting Shirley Chisholm.

People cursed at her, she said.

People told her that she was no good.

People wagged their fingers in her face.

"I don't want to hear what you've done in the past," Shirley said people told her. "I don't want to hear what committees you're on down there in Washington in that House of Representatives. I want me a job, Shirley Chisholm. Get me a job."

Shirley couldn't lie to them, couldn't lie to herself. She faced the truth: *"I cannot deliver,"* she told Hacker.

That interview was held in December 1982.

The place: Shirley's office in the Rayburn Building, about a six-minute walk from the Capitol.

At the time of the interview, Shirley's office was a sad sight. Behind her desk, wrote Hacker, "nails protrude from the blue walls where photographs and certificates once hung; cabinets stand with their doors ajar, ready to be stripped of their accumulation of books."

In the waiting room one staffer was trying to fit into Shirley's already jam-packed schedule an interview request from a German TV show. That staffer told Hacker that ever since Shirley announced that she was leaving Congress, droves of reporters had been pouring into the office.

★ ★ ★

By then, like the rest of the nation, Shirley had lived through the Watergate scandal, named after D.C.'s Watergate complex. It's where the Democratic National Committee was headquartered in 1972. During the election season Nixon operatives had broken into the place to bug the telephones.

The cover-up was worse than the crime. The scandal ultimately led to President Richard Nixon's downfall. Rather than be impeached, Nixon did something no other U.S. president had ever done. On August 9, 1974, he resigned, handing over the reins to Vice President Gerald Ford.

During Ford's presidency the U.S. economy tanked. Americans experienced the worst economic downturn since the Great Depression that hit when Shirley was a child—and so no wonder that many of her constituents were having such a tough time.

Things remained grim economically for many Americans under President Jimmy Carter, former governor of Georgia, who left the Oval Office in 1981.

The next president was former actor and former California governor Ronald Reagan. Back in 1964, he came into national prominence while campaigning for Barry Goldwater.

Fighting Shirley Chisholm raged against the Reagan Administration when she spoke with Hacker. "All these millionaire gentlemen who make up President Reagan's cabinet are cut out of the same bolt of cloth," she said. "How in heaven's name do they know anything about the so-called underdogs of America? What do they know of the poor white person in the hills of Pennsylvania, the black people suffering in the deltas of the Mississippi, the senior citizens worrying month to month whether they're going to lose their only means of support in the twilight of their lives?"

And Shirley wasn't about to stay in Congress just to hold on to a very good salary: "Sure I could sit here for another term, collect my $60,000 a year and hope the Reagan Administration is turned out. But I don't have the stomach for it."

But Shirley's inability to really deliver for her constituents and her frustration with the Reagan Administration weren't the only factors in her decision to quit Congress. Many prominent, progressive New Yorkers had soured on her. They didn't think her voice was needed.

A few years before she announced that she was leaving Congress, New York City's *Village Voice* ran a long, scathing article titled "Chisholm's Compromise: Politics and the Art of Self-Interest." It was written by Shirley's former UDC colleague Andy Cooper and by Wayne Barrett. Their article charged that Shirley wasn't as "unbossed and unbought" as she claimed to be and that she had "made a career of compromise." They cited numerous times when she failed to back liberal and progressive candidates—including Black ones and feminist women. Instead, she endorsed establishment candidates: those backed by powerful Democrats, and often white.

Many New Yorkers were furious with Shirley, for example, when she turned her back on Percy Sutton. In 1977, when Sutton threw his hat into the ring to be the Big Apple's first Black mayor, Shirley refused to endorse him—someone with whom she'd worked in the New York State Assembly, someone who had raised money for her campaign when she ran for Congress in 1968, someone who had been among her staunchest supporters when she ran for president.

Said Sutton to Cooper and Barrett: "I believed I could count on her support. I just don't understand Shirley Chisholm."

"Chisholm's Compromise" essentially declared that Shirley was no longer a woman of the people.

But when it comes to politics nothing is simple.

In her 2013 book, *Shirley Chisholm: Catalyst for Change,* Barbara Winslow, founder of Brooklyn College's Shirley Chisholm Project, felt that much of Cooper and Barrett's critique was spot on. But Winslow, with the benefit of hindsight, also pointed out that, in all likelihood, had it not been for the support of powerful Democrats, Shirley would not have been in Congress as long as she was. "The Democratic Party machine's support of Chisholm enabled her to stay in Congress by protecting her from primary challenges. In return for her loyalty to the machine, she could continue to be outspoken and provocative."

What's more, Winslow maintained that Cooper and Barrett didn't truly "take into account the precariousness of Chisholm's political position"—that Shirley had to "battle politically in a white man's political world, where daggers were out at all times."

★ ★ ★

Shirley also had a deeply personal reason for leaving Congress. During her talk with the *Philadelphia Inquirer*'s Hacker, she brought out from her wallet a photograph of her and Arthur. It was from their honeymoon.

Shirley kissed the photo, then told Hacker about the strain she'd been under ever since June 1979, when Arthur was in a terrible car accident.

Both arms broken.

Both legs broken.

Chest crushed.

Arthur spent about a year in the hospital. After that, he got about in a wheelchair for another six months. Not being able to be constantly by his side took a toll on Shirley. "For an entire year," she said, "I left Congress each day and ran to my apartment, afraid I couldn't get the key in the door fast enough before I'd start crying." Tears of guilt.

Months before, Shirley had told a different journalist that she had come close to taking a leave of absence, but Arthur said, nonsense. "You go and drown yourself in your work," he told her. "I will make it."

And he did. When Hacker spoke with Shirley, Arthur was getting around under his own steam, albeit with a limp.

Hacker's article also revealed that in leaving Congress after 14 years of service, Shirley wasn't leaving the fight for a better America. She'd be fighting on a different front. She was returning to her first profession.

Come February 1983, Shirley would begin teaching a few days a week on women's studies, politics, and race at Mount Holyoke College in Hadley, Massachusetts. Besides teaching, Shirley planned to "write, and play her piano, and eat dinner with her husband, and dance," reported Hacker.

─── ★ ★ ★ ───

In their home in Williamsville, New York, near Niagara Falls, Shirley didn't have many more years to eat dinner with Arthur, or breakfast or lunch for that matter. He died on August 18, 1986, the day after his 70th birthday.

In 1987 Shirley, age 62, stepped down from teaching at Mount Holyoke. But she remained a much in-demand speaker. She said yes to scores of invitations to speak on race relations, on women's rights, on the need for multicultural education, on any cause she believed needed a champion—a voice.

She didn't remain alive with activity for many more years, however. In 1991 Shirley pretty much retired from public life. She left the Northeast for Florida. She lived first in Palm Coast, then in Ormond Beach.

In 1993, two years after she moved to Florida, President Bill Clinton nominated Shirley to be the U.S. ambassador to Jamaica, but she declined for health reasons.

It was also in 1993 that Shirley, along with 34 other pioneers in an array of fields, was inducted into the National Women's Hall of Fame.

Though ailing, Shirley still had the strength to work on a third book. It was a book about sexism and racism in politics, a book in which readers could learn, she told a reporter, the "true story of how racism and sexism befuddles even the best of people."

Shirley's working title for this book that was never published was *The Illusion of Inclusion.*

It was a book she planned to dedicate to the American people.

EPILOGUE

SATURDAY, JANUARY 1, 2005.

Ormond Beach, Florida.

Following several strokes, Fighting Shirley Chisholm, who had definitely made something of herself, who had definitely used that mighty brain of hers as her papa had urged, died at age 80.

In the days immediately following her death, Shirley was once again in the news.

"Mrs. Chisholm was an outspoken, steely educator-turned-politician who shattered racial and gender barriers as she became a national symbol of liberal politics in the 1960's and 1970's," said the *New York Times*'s obituary.

Said the United Kingdom's *Guardian:* "Throughout her life she had stuck to the philosophy she spelled out in one of her speeches. 'You don't make progress by standing on the sidelines, whimpering and complaining. You make progress by implementing ideas.'"

"She was a pioneer and a patriot, undeterred by the prospect of failure or by what people thought about her," stated a writer with the *Chicago Tribune.*

"I don't think there's anyone on the American scene today who played the role Shirley Chisholm played." That was legendary civil rights activist Congressman John Lewis of Georgia.

"Perhaps if there was not a Shirley Chisholm, I would not be a member of the United States Congress," said Julia Carson. She was Indianapolis,

Indiana's first woman and first Black representative. Carson and 84 other women made up nearly 16 percent of the U.S. legislature.

Sadly, with the passage of time, many people forgot or were never taught about Fighting Shirley Chisholm, who paved the way for people like Julia Carson and who, with her 1972 run for the presidency, paved the way for a host of politicians who weren't white males to seek the highest office in the land.

They include, of course, the nation's first Black president, Democrat Barack Hussein Obama, first elected in 2008. In 2015 President Obama honored Shirley with the highest award a president can bestow upon a civilian, the Presidential Medal of Freedom.

Then, in 2016, Democrat Hillary Rodham Clinton, for whom Shirley also paved the way, became the first woman to clinch the presidential nomination of a major U.S. political party.

Clinton lost the election to Republican Donald J. Trump.

★ ★ ★

Three years into Trump's presidency, during a time when the people of the United States were deeply divided over a range of issues, from immigration and the Black Lives Matter movement to climate change …

The *New York Times* had a headline that warmed many hearts, buoyed many spirits.

"2019 Belongs to Shirley Chisholm."

That year marked the 50th anniversary of Shirley becoming the first Black woman in the U.S. House of Representatives. Tributes, celebrations, and remembrances of this pioneer abounded. Especially in the city where she was born on a partly cloudy Sunday 95 years earlier.

In April 2019 the She Built NYC commission unveiled a rendering of a 40-foot-tall steel monument to Shirley Chisholm to grace an entrance to

Brooklyn's Prospect Park.

On July 2 the first section of Brooklyn's 407-acre Shirley Chisholm State Park opened.

Said New York's Governor Andrew Cuomo: "Shirley Chisholm fought to improve the health and wellness of underserved communities, a legacy we are carrying on through the Vital Brooklyn Initiative, so we are proud to dedicate this park in memory of her leadership and accomplishments."

The year 2019 also saw an abundance of T-shirts, coffee mugs, and other items sporting the image of Fighting Shirley Chisholm.

Why all this Shirley Chisholm mania?

Writer John Stanton said it best when he told the *New York Times,* "People want heroes right now."

Among the many people who had long regarded Shirley as a hero was Kamala Harris. In 2020 she was elected the United States' first woman, first Black American, and first South Asian American vice president.

A few days before Inauguration Day 2021 vice president–elect Harris tweeted, "Shirley Chisholm created a path for me and for so many others."

★ ★ ★

IF THEY DON'T GIVE YOU A SEAT AT THE TABLE, BRING IN A FOLDING CHAIR.
—SHIRLEY CHISHOLM

AUTHOR'S NOTE

WRITING A BIOGRAPHY OF SHIRLEY CHISHOLM WAS A
natural fit for me, a native New Yorker who lived for a time as a tot on
Clifton Place in Bed-Stuy, who spent her wonder years in Harlem and
did the rest of her growing up in the Bronx.

I was a kid when Shirley ran for the New York State Assembly in
1964 and when she ran for Congress in 1968. I was a teenager when she
ran for president in 1972.

What I most remember about her during those days was her clear,
clipped, bold voice. I was short on details, but I knew that she was a
phenomenon, a force. When she ran for president, I remember being
boggled, astonished—thinking, *Wow!*, and feeling so proud! For a Black
girl to see a Black woman embark on such an endeavor—go where
no Black woman had ever gone before—how could I not feel a surge
of pride?

When Shirley left Congress in 1982, though I still didn't know all
that much about her, I definitely understood that she was among the
Black women who paved the way for me: for me to not hold back from
any endeavor, any passion because I was Black and female.

In a way, with *Speak Up, Speak Out!* I'm saying, "Thank you, Shirley
Chisholm!"

★ ★ ★

While researching Shirley's extraordinary life, I discovered other Black
female political trailblazers from my hometown—women who, in a way,

paved the way for Shirley.

For example, there was Bed-Stuy activist Ada Jackson, known as the "Fighting Lady of Brooklyn." In 1944, when Shirley was in college, Jackson ran (unsuccessfully) to represent the 17th AD in the New York State Assembly. She was the American Labor Party candidate, as she was when she ran again (and lost again) in 1946.

There was also the Republican Maude Richardson, co-founder of the CBCC of which Shirley was a member. Like Jackson, twice in the 1940s Richardson ran unsuccessfully to represent the 17th AD in Albany. In 1950 she became the 17th AD's first Black co-leader.

Another example: In 1954, when Shirley was at the start of her career with Mac Holder's Bedford-Stuyvesant Political League, former singer and dancer Bessie Buchanan, Democrat, became the first Black woman elected to the New York State Assembly, representing a district in Harlem.

By the way, when Shirley was elected to the New York State Assembly in 1964, another Black woman, civil rights attorney Constance Baker Motley, made history as the first Black woman elected to the New York State Senate. But she wasn't there for long. This daughter of Caribbean immigrants resigned in early 1965 after the New York City Council tapped her to fill a vacancy for Manhattan Borough president, a first for a woman. And in 1966 Motley made history again—the first Black woman federal judge.

Before I began work on *Speak Up, Speak Out!*, I knew that Shirley wasn't the first Black person or the first woman to run for president— seeking to make that someday come. I knew, for example, of the radical white woman Victoria Woodhull, who in 1872—nearly 50 years before women had the vote nationwide—ran for president as the candidate of the Equal Rights Party (which nominated Frederick Douglass for

VP, but he never accepted). I also knew about Dick Gregory, Black activist-comedian, who in 1968 was a write-in presidential candidate for the Freedom and Peace Party.

But I didn't know about George Edwin Taylor. In 1904 this Black newspaperman and community organizer then of Ottumwa, Iowa, ran for president as the candidate of the National Negro Liberty Party (also known as the National Liberty Party).

Nor had I heard of the white woman Margaret Chase Smith, the first woman to serve in both the House of Representatives (1940-49) and the U.S. Senate (1949-1973). In 1964 Smith sought to be the Republican Party's presidential candidate.

Exploring Shirley's life opened me up to so much history!

But there were frustrations along the way. COVID-19 lockdowns prevented me from accessing certain material, such as all of Shirley's papers at Brooklyn College. But I did my best to make the most of what I could access, from her memoirs and other books to digitized newspapers and immigration records to other documents. These included censuses and her beloved dad's World War II draft registration card where I learned details like the name of the bag company for which he worked, and where he claimed that he was born not in British Guiana, but in Barbados.

Barbados: Where his dear Shirls once fed chickens and other animals, hauled water from a well, enjoyed so many hot, sunny days, stunning white-sand beaches, clear-clear turquoise water, and palm trees sent swaying by a breeze.

Barbados: Where her grandmother told her time and again, "Child, you've got to face things with courage."

That is something a grown-up Shirls most certainly did.

—*Tonya Bolden, New York City, 2020*

★ ★ ★ ★ ★ ★ ★ ★ ★ ★

NOTES & SOURCES

NOTES
Please see Selected Sources for complete citations of books and the DVD.

Epigraph
10 "If Harriet Tubman . . .": Metcalf, *Up From Within*, 113. **10** "I'd like them to say . . .": Susan Brownmiller, "This Is Fighting Shirley Chisholm," *New York Times Magazine*, April 13, 1969, 33.

Prologue
11 Announcement: "Shirley Chisholm Presidential Candidacy Announcement," American Rhetoric, https://www.american rhetoric.com/speeches/shirleychisholmpresidentialcandidacyannouncement.htm. **12** "a breath-taking expedition . . .": Mary McGrory, "Her Program Is Chisholm," *Sunday Star*, January 30, 1972, F1. **12** Weather on January 25, 1972, and on November 30, 1924: *New York Times*, January 25,1972, 1; and *New York Times*, November 30, 1924, 1.

Chapter 1: Use It
13 "You must make something . . . use it": Chisholm, *Unbought and Unbossed*, 33. **14** Brooklyn's population circa 1923: Wilder, *A Covenant With Color*, table 6.1, 118. **16** "GIRL . . .": *Brooklyn Daily Eagle*, January 2, 1924, 15. **16** Black women domestic workers: Gallagher, *Black Women and Politics*, 208, note 8.

Chapter 2: With Courage
17 "early in 1928 . . . the *Vulcania*": Chisholm, *Unbought and Unbossed*, 25. **17** On date of departure: Shirley stated that her mom stayed with her girls in Barbados for six months to help them adjust to island life. But records show that Ruby returned to the States in early May 1929. "Early in 1928" until early May 1929 is over a year. **17–18** "straight-backed . . . warmth and love" and "The night noises . . .": Chisholm, *Unbought and Unbossed*, 26. **18** "Child, you've got to . . .": Kathy Hacker, "Chisholm Looks Back in Anger," *Philadelphia Inquirer*, December 13, 1982, 4C. **18** "When you started school . . .": Muriel Forde in Lynch, *Chisholm '72—Unbought and Unbossed*, DVD.

Chapter 3: Our Places in the World
21 "New York's rawest . . . damp sadness": Kazin, *A Walker in the City*, 12. **21** "Like the cars . . . in the back": Chisholm, *Unbought and Unbossed*, 30. **22** "poised, modest . . .": Chisholm, *Unbought and Unbossed*, 31. **22–23** "Ruby . . . not island kids": Chisholm, *Unbought and Unbossed*, 38. **23** "Papa read everything . . ." and "tireless talker": Chisholm, *Unbought and Unbossed*, 32. **23** "He had to have his shoes . . .": Chisholm, *Unbought and Unbossed*, 33. **24** "Luckily someone . . . age-grade level": Chisholm, *Unbought and Unbossed*, 34. **24** Near-genius IQ: Stephan Lesher, "The Short, Unhappy Life of Black Presidential Politics, 1972," *New York Times*, June 25, 1972, https://www.nytimes.com/1972/06/25/archives/the-short-unhappy-life-of-black-presidential-politics-1972-black.html. **26** "rough and callused . . .": Chisholm, *Unbought and Unbossed*, 37.

Chapter 4: Had to Read
27 "By the time . . . with my mouth": Chisholm, *Unbought and Unbossed*, 23. **27** "a leader of her people": Tom Tiede, "First Negro Woman Elected to Congress a Political Trail Blazer," *Iowa City Press-Citizen*, November 20, 1968, 2D. **27** "He believed in me . . . you'll do it": Joy Miller, "Shirley Chisholm Blazes New Trails in Politics," *Sunday Call-Chronicle*, January 5, 1969, A14. **27** "a bun" and "We had to read": Chisholm, *Unbought and Unbossed*, 37. **28** "got going . . . to go home": Chisholm, *Unbought and Unbossed*, 36. **29** WWII headlines: June 15, 1940, 1; September 11, 1940, 1; April 7, 1941, 1; and February 24, 1942, 1. All in the *New York Times*. **30** Brooklyn College entrance exam, GPA requirements, and its student body: http://www.brooklyn.cuny.edu/bc/ahp/Students.html; Winslow, *Shirley Chisholm*, 21, 22; and "Brooklyn College Student Enrollment Analysis Headcount Enrollment By Year, Since 1930," http://www.brooklyn.cuny.edu/bc/offices/avpbandp/ipra/enrollment/HeadcountEnrollmentSince1930.pdf. **31** "There was no other . . . too expensive": Chisholm, *Unbought and Unbossed*, 41. **31** Interest in acting and "I come alive . . . when I dance": Gloria Negri, "A Pepperpot for Congress," *Boston Globe*, November 8, 1968, 15; and Metcalf, *Up From Within*, 115. **31** "bump up . . .": Chisholm, *Unbought and Unbossed*, 40.

Chapter 5: Alive With Activity
32 "miracles in a metropolis . . .": "Trees Grow in Brooklyn and College Boasts 1005," *Brooklyn Eagle*, September 1, 1946, 13. **32** "alive with activity": Chisholm, *Unbought and Unbossed*, 40. **32** Posters and flyers at Brooklyn College: Presidential Files, Brooklyn College, http://academic.brooklyn.cuny.edu/english/melani/bc/gideonse_files/index.html. **32** Ipothia's aims: "Ipothia Sorority at Boro College," *Amsterdam News*, December 23, 1944, 17. **33** "looked at my people . . . limited": Chisholm, *Unbought and Unbossed*, 42. **33** Steingut's sentiments and "Uh huh—that's what you think": Camille Cosby, "Excerpts From the National Visionary Leadership Project, May 7, 2002," https://awpc.cattcenter.iastate.edu/2017/03/09/excerpts-from-the-national-visionary-leadership-project-may-7-2002/. **33** "I painted posters . . .": Chisholm, *Unbought and Unbossed*, 43. **34** Cost of home and "a really remarkable . . .": Chisholm, *Unbought and Unbossed*, 45. Later neighborhood boundary changes put the

136

house in Crown Heights. **34–35** "I didn't look old enough . . ." and "At least . . . my size": Chisholm, *Unbought and Unbossed,* 45. **35–36** Shirley's meeting Conrad and her earlier heartbreak and depression: Chisholm, *Unbought and Unbossed,* 62–63. **36** Conrad's background: Dolores Barclay, "She's 'Star'—He's Happy," *Evening Press* (Binghamton, New York), March 1, 1972, 14C.

Chapter 6: Two Things

37 "You ought to go into politics" and "Proffy . . . I'm a woman": Chisholm, *Unbought and Unbossed,* 43. In her autobiography Chisholm said that Warsoff was blind. In several articles about him from the 1930s, 1940s, and 1950s I found no mention that he, a captain in the Air Force's Judge Advocate General's Office during World War II, was born blind or lost his sight at some point. **38** Steve Carney: In her autobiography Chisholm wrote that during this period (the 1940s) Steve's brother, Vince, was district leader. Vince didn't become district leader until the 1950s. **38** "He is conspicuously absent . . .": *Amsterdam News,* February 1, 1947, 14. **38** "with his flunkies . . .": Chisholm, *Unbought and Unbossed,* 46. **38** "Such questions were unwelcome": Chisholm, *Unbought and Unbossed,* 47. **39** "shrewdest, toughest . . .": Chisholm, *Unbought and Unbossed,* 48. **39** "Why should we . . . ," "Women are the backbone . . . ," and "It will stay out . . .": Chisholm, *Unbought and Unbossed,* 50. **40** Flagg's primary and general election wins: Harold H. Harris, "Politics and People," *Brooklyn Eagle,* October 21, 1953, 2; and "Flagg First of Race Elected to Bench Here," *Brooklyn Eagle,* November 4, 1953, 1. **40–41** Shirley as first VP of BSPL and as VP of 17th AD Democratic Club: "Holder League Prexy for the Third Term," January 28, 1956, 20; and Daphne Sheppard, "King's Diary," January 9, 1957, 19. Both in the *Amsterdam News.* **41** Women's Council breakfast and fundraising for Stuyvesant Community Center: "Unsung Heroines," January 25, 1958, 10; "Women's Council Fetes Six at Breakfast," February 8, 1958, 19; and "Mrs. Chisholm Heads Drive," December 6, 1958, 20. All in the *Amsterdam News.* **41** "there was nothing . . ." and "had a right . . .": Chisholm, *Unbought and Unbossed,* 55–56. **42** "often unfair . . . shrewd cookie": David English, et al., *Divided They Stand,* 149. **42–43** Need for day care: Dolores Waldorf, "Day Care for Young Conference Subject," *Oakland Tribune,* November 21, 1959, 10B. **43** "drawn back into politics": Chisholm, *Unbought and Unbossed,* 65.

Chapter 7: Battling for a Better Bed-Stuy

44 "to do what . . .": Chisholm, *Unbought and Unbossed,* 65. **45** UDC's October 1960 rally: "Hedgeman to Help Push Registration," *Amsterdam News,* October 1, 1960, 21. **45** Bed-Stuy's population circa 1930: Bureau of Community Statistical Services, Research Department, *Brooklyn Communities,* 100. **45** Bed-Stuy's population circa 1960: David English, et al., *Divided They Stand,* 149. **46** "airmail express": Purnell, *Fighting Jim Crow,* 137. **46** Sanitation services in Bed-Stuy and Marine Park: Purnell, *Fighting Jim Crow,* 133–134, 136. **46** "not rest": *Amsterdam News,* February 20, 1960, 21. **47** "We made a lot of noise": Chisholm, *Unbought and Unbossed,* 65. **47** CBCC agenda Shirley drafted: Woodsworth, *Battle for Bed-Stuy,* 100. **48** Purpose of the jobs center and its opening: Woodsworth, *Battle for Bed-Stuy,* 119, and "Boro Labor Office Opens With a Band," *Amsterdam News,* July 6, 1963, 23. **48–49** Mayor Wagner's speech: Woodsworth, *Battle for Bed-Stuy,* 120. **50** "Segregation now . . .": "Inaugural Address of Governor George C. Wallace, January 14, 1963," Montgomery, Alabama, Alabama Department of Archives and History, http://digital.archives.alabama.gov/cdm/ref/collection/voices/id/2952. **50** "bundle of T-shirts . . .": Anthony Burton, "U.S. in All-Out Hunt as Killing Stirs Mississippi," *New York Daily News,* June 13, 1963, 3. **50–51** "Freedom March": *Amsterdam News,* September 28, 1963, 50. **51** "Lighted Candle" memorial: "Jones' 'Candle in Window' Idea Has Backing of Leaders," *Amsterdam News,* November 30, 1963, 19.

Chapter 8: Key Woman

53 "didn't want to see me . . .": Chisholm, *Unbought and Unbossed,* 69. **53** "By then . . . get elected": Chisholm, *Unbought and Unbossed,* 69. **53** "If you need to have a discussion . . .": Metcalf, *Up From Within,* 119–120. **54** Shirley on the ballot: "2-Borough Hopefuls File for Primaries," *New York Daily News,* April 28, 1964, B3. **54** "Pioneer": "First Bklyn Negro Woman Running for the Assembly," *Amsterdam News,* May 9, 1964, 33. **54** "stunning in a black velvet . . .": Marjorie Ison, "Across the Brooklyn Bridge," *New Pittsburgh Courier,* February 8, 1964, 5. **54** "Elect me to dramatize . . .": Winslow, *Shirley Chisholm,* 45. **55** "Young woman . . . for men" and "I handled . . . elected office": Chisholm, *Unbought and Unbossed,* 70–71, 71. **55** "what to run my campaign with": Chisholm, *Unbought and Unbossed,* 70. **56** "We all got . . . her backbone": Gallagher, *Black Women and Politics,* 165. **56** June 2, 1964, election results: Gallagher, *Black Women and Politics,* 235, note 28. **56** "unconditional war . . . prevent it": Lyndon B. Johnson, State of the Union Address, January 8, 1964, University of Virginia, Miller Center, https://millercenter.org/the-presidency/presidential-speeches/january-8-1964-state-union. **57** "the battle to build the Great Society": Lyndon B. Johnson, Commencement Speech at the University of Michigan, May 22, 1964, Teaching American History, https://teachingamericanhistory.org/library/document/great-society-speech/. **57** School boycott: Leonard Buder, "Pickets Peaceful," *New York Times,* February 4, 1964, 1. **57–58** "Law of the Land": *Amsterdam News,* September 5, 1964, 46. **58–59** "Killer Cops . . . Nostrand Avenue": "Cops Halt Bdfd-Stuyvesant Riot, CORE Sets More Demonstrations," *Amsterdam News,* July 25, 1964, 25. **59** "What is the sense of . . . the government?": Chisholm, *Unbought and Unbossed,* 157. **59** Wagner's grant to YIA: Charles G. Bennett, "Brooklyn Antipoverty Program Is Set," *New York Times,* July 26, 1964, 42. **59–60** Jobs for young people: Woodsworth, *Battle for Bed-Stuy,* 145. **60** LBJ's worry: Jeremy D. Mayer, "LBJ Fights the White Backlash: The Racial Politics of the 1964 Presidential Campaign," *Prologue,* Spring 2001, vol. 33, no. 1, https://www.archives.gov/publications/prologue/2001/spring/lbj-and-white-backlash-1.html. **60** Goldwater's blame game: Michael W. Flamm, "The Original Long, Hot Summer," *New York Times,* July 15, 2014, https://www.nytimes.com/2014/07/16/opinion/16Flamm.html.

Chapter 9: *Paso a Paso*

62 Election results: "How Negro Candidates Fared," *Amsterdam News,* November 7, 1964, 3. **62–63** "her feathered Robin Hood cap . . . lejos": Daphne Sheppard, "The Lady Is Also a First," *Amsterdam News,* November 7, 1964, 27. **63** "I collapsed screaming . . .": Chisholm, *Unbought and Unbossed,* 72. **63** "I almost went to pieces": Joy Miller, "Shirley Chisholm Blazes New Trails in Politics," *Sunday Call-Chronicle,* January 5, 1969, A14. **63** "My election would . . .": Chisholm, *Unbought and Unbossed,* 72. **63** "making white sand castles . . .": Daphne Sheppard, "Kings Diary," *Amsterdam News,* December 12, 1964, 31.

Chapter 10: The Pepperpot

64 "At first glance . . .": Theresa St. John, "With History Comes Hauntings—The New York State Capitol Has Its Fair Share," July 2, 2018, https://www.milesgeek.com/hauntings-new-york-state-capitol. **64** "a testament to the state's . . .": Jesse McKinley, "A Jewel in Albany Regains Its Luster," *New York Times,* March 9, 2013, https://www.nytimes.com/2013/03/10/nyregion/albanys-capitol-building-newly-renovated-shines-anew.html. **64** Makeup of 175th New York State Legislature: "Legal Beagles Dominate New Legislative Roster," *Rockland County Journal-News,* January 4, 1965, 2. **65** "the Speaker had even more authority . . .": Dinkins, *A Mayor's Life,* 59. **65** "No one was paying . . . a newcomer": Chisholm, *Unbought and Unbossed,* 74. **65** "political suicide": Chisholm, *Unbought and Unbossed,* 75. **66** "made persistent . . .": Chisholm, *Unbought and Unbossed,* 80. **67** Bills on day care centers, police officers, and unemployment insurance for domestic workers: Assembly Bill #1932, introduced February 10, 1965; Assembly Bill #2553, introduced February 17, 1965; and Assembly Bill #2558, introduced February 17, 1965. **67** "Every black woman . . . got nothing": Metcalf, *Up From Within,* 121. **67** "human relations," "a dangerous step," and "It is a bill . . .": "Legislature OKs Requiring 'Human Relations' Teaching," *Star-Gazette and Advertiser* (Elmira, New York), April 16, 1965, other editions, 4. **67** "the pepperpot . . . breathe fire": Gloria Negri, "A Pepperpot for Congress," *Boston Evening Globe,* November 8, 1968, 1. **67–68** Bills on pre-K, courses in race relations or black history, and high school courses on alcohol and drugs: Assembly Bill #1181, introduced January 5, 1966; Assembly Bill #4531, introduced by David Dinkins, February 15, 1966; and Assembly Bill #1240, introduced January 4, 1967. **68** Brooklyn Children's Museum: "Seek City Support for Child's Museum," *Amsterdam News,* April 8, 1967, 24; and Assembly Bill #2964, introduced January 25, 1967. **68** Number of bills introduced and co-sponsored: *New York Legislative Record and Index* (Albany, NY: The Legislative Index Company, 1965, 1966, 1967, 1968), 1095, 1119, 60, 71–72. In her autobiography Chisholm wrote that she sponsored 50 bills and that eight passed: Chisholm, *Unbought and Unbossed,* 78–79. **68–69** Incognito visits to schools: Metcalf, *Up From Within,* 121. **69** Midnight March: Dinkins, *A Mayor's Life,* 60. **69–70** Boys' Club fundraiser, luncheon, appreciation dinner, and cleanup drive: "Youths Launch Drive," February 27, 1965, 25; Daphne Sheppard, "Zeta Sorority Cites Outstanding Women," March 27, 1965, 31; "Community Salutes Woman Lawmaker," April 27, 1965, 30; and "5-Block Clean Up Operation," June 26, 1965, 32. All in the *Amsterdam News.* **70** A Reader from Brooklyn's letter and Shirley's response: "Additional Letters," August 21, 1965, 14; and "Replies to Critic," August 28, 1965, 14. Both in the *Amsterdam News.* **71** "David, I'm going to . . .": David Dinkins, "Dinkins on Chisholm and the Changing Political Scene," *Columbia Magazine,* Spring 2005, http://www.columbia.edu/cu/alumni/Magazine/Spring2005/dinkins.html.

Chapter 11: Fighting Shirley Chisholm

72 Women in the House by 1968: Wikipedia, https://en.wikipedia.org/wiki/Women_in_the_United_States_House_of_Representatives#Number_of_women_in_the_United_States_House_of_Representatives_and_Senate_by_Congress. **73** "tortuous, artificial . . .": Thomas J. Lueck, "Andrew W. Cooper, 74, Pioneering Journalist," *New York Times,* January 30, 2002, B7. **74** Shirley's nonresponse to Cooper: Dawkins, *City Son,* 52. **74** "Mrs. Shirley Chisholm has already . . ." and "I was excited . . . my independence and courage": Daphne Sheppard, "CNC Chooses Chisholm Congressional Choice," *Amsterdam News,* December 30, 1967, 19. **75** "soul-searching": "Holder Chisholm Coordinator," *Amsterdam News,* March 23, 1968, 58. **75** "In the black neighborhood . . .": Chisholm, *Unbought and Unbossed,* 86. **75** "Sock it to 'em, Shirley!": Dee Wedemeyer, "Brooklyn Elects First Negro Congresswoman," *Anniston Star,* November 6, 1968, 6A. **75** Registered voters: Metcalf, *Up From Within,* 122. **76** Conrad's claim: Metcalf, *Up From Within,* 127. **76** Letter to Rockefeller: George Barner, "Black Legislators Bitter Over Cuts in Medicaid," *Amsterdam News,* March 16, 1968, 43. **77** Robert F. Kennedy, "Statement on Assassination of Martin Luther King, Jr., Indianapolis, Indiana, April 4, 1968," John F. Kennedy Presidential Library and Museum, https://www.jfklibrary.org/learn/about-jfk/the-kennedy-family/robert-f-kennedy/robert-f-kennedy-speeches/statement-on-assassination-of-martin-luther-king-jr-indianapolis-indiana-april-4-1968. **78** "the loss . . . greater still": Chisholm, *The Good Fight,* 96. **78** Final vote tally: Daphne Sheppard, "Bed-Stuy Primary Round-Up Shows Sweep by New Breed," *Amsterdam News,* June 29, 1968, 21. **78** Outfit and "aware of the barriers . . . help of the people": Daphne Sheppard, "Chisholm, Stewart, Thompson in Upset Primary Victories," *Amsterdam News,* June 22, 1968, 23.

Chapter 12: Tough, Baby

79 "Farmer's Chances Are Good": *New Pittsburgh Courier,* June 1, 1968, 3. **79** "Where's Mrs. Chisholm?" and **80** "Ladies and gentlemen . . .": Chisholm, *Unbought and Unbossed,* 89–90. **80** Campaign pledges: Chisholm, *Unbought and Unbossed,* 110. **80** Cost of Vietnam war and American deaths in it in 1968: "1968 in the Vietnam War," Wikipedia, https://en.wikipedia.org/wiki/1968_in_the_Vietnam_War and "Year of Death," Vietnam War U.S. Military Fatal Casualty Statistics, National Archives, https://www.archives.gov/research/military/vietnam-war/casualty-statistics. **80–81** "been in the driver's seat . . . little schoolteacher": "Chisholm, Shirley Anita," History, Art & Archives, United States House of Representatives, https://history.house.gov/People/Listing/C/CHISHOLM,-Shirley-Anita-(C000371)/. **81** "It doesn't matter what you think . . .": Dee Wedemeyer, "Brooklyn Elects First Negro Congresswoman," *Anniston Star,* November 6, 1968, 6A. **81** "Who are you? . . . the Assembly": Chisholm, *Unbought and Unbossed,* 88. **82** "I told Shirley . . . of the pyramid": Metcalf, *Up From Within,* 129. **82** Registered Democrats and the percentage of Puerto Ricans in the 12th CD: "Chisholm, Shirley Anita," History, Art & Archives, United States House of Representatives. Cited above. **82** "If I ever had any doubts . . .": Chisholm, *Unbought and Unbossed,* 90. **83** Backing of labor: Daphne Sheppard, "Chisholm Gets Labor Backing for Congress," *Amsterdam News,* November 2, 1968, 27. **83** Headlines on Shirley's victory: Dee Wedemeyer, "Brooklyn Elects First Negro Congresswoman," *Anniston Star,* November 6, 1968, 6A; "First Negro Woman Wins Congressional Seat," *Daily Tribune* (Wisconsin Rapids, Wisconsin), November 6, 1968, 20; and Richard L. Madden, "Mrs. Chisholm Defeats Farmer, Is First Negro Woman in House," *New York Times,* November 6, 1968, 1. **83** Election results: Chisholm, *Unbought and Unbossed,* 94. **83** "My dear friends . . . United State Congress": Walter Ray Watson, "A Look Back on Shirley Chisholm's Historic 1968 House Victory," *Morning Edition,* NPR, https://www.npr.org/2018/11/06/664617076/a-look-back-on-shirley-chisholm-s-historic-1968-house-victory.

83 Year of the Woman: Judy Klemesrud, "1968: For Women, It Was a Year Marked by Numerous 'Firsts,' " *New York Times,* January 1, 1969, 25. **84** "Friends, relatives, well-wishers . . . freshness": Dolores Alexander, "Representative Chisholm: The First to Win," *Oakland Tribune,* December 2, 1968, 25. **84** "My mouth" and "cheerful duplex": Beatrice Berg, "Shirley Chisholm: Congressional First," *Courier-Journal & Times* (Louisville, Kentucky), December 15, 1968, D14. **84–85** Gala at the Hotel St. George: Daphne Sheppard, "1000 Honor Shirley at Victory Salute Gala," *Amsterdam News,* December 28, 1968, 29. **85** "Poor to Honor Shirley": *Amsterdam News,* December 21, 1968, 31.

Chapter 13: Doing Her Thing

86 "black woman congressman": Winslow, *Shirley Chisholm,* 56. **86** "curiosity about how . . .": Chisholm, *Unbought and Unbossed,* 98. **87** "Mrs. Chisholm . . . about something, you do it": Chisholm, *Unbought and Unbossed,* 99. **87** "A first-term congresswoman . . . kill the assignment": "House Decision Upset," *Spokane Daily Chronicle,* January 29, 1969, 20. **87** "There are a lot more veterans . . .": Chisholm, *Unbought and Unbossed,* 103. **88** Insults from southern congressmen: Sheila Moran, "Shirley Chisholm: 'No One Can Crush My Spirit,' " *Danville Register,* April 13, 1972, 8C. **88** Robbery: Malvina Stephenson and Vera Glaser, "Tasteful Thief Robs 'Fighting Shirley,' " *St. Petersburg Times,* January 15, 1969, 51. **88–89** Speech against defense spending: "An Appraisal of the Conflict in Vietnam," *Congressional Record—House,* vol. 115, part 6, March 26, 1969, 7765. **89** Cuts to Head Start: Betty James, "OEO to Cut 1,000 Pupils in Head Start," *Evening Star,* March 14, 1969, 1. **90** "You know, she's crazy!": Chisholm, *Unbought and Unbossed,* 114. **90** "student groups . . . struck a responsive chord": Chisholm, *Unbought and Unbossed,* 114–115.

Chapter 14: Outrageous

91 MLK birthday, Social Security increase, and benefits for cops and firefighters: *Congressional Record Index,* vol. 115, part 31, January 3, 1969, to December 23, 1969 (Washington, DC: U.S. Government Printing Office, 1969), 227. **91–92** Speech on ERA: "Equal Rights for Women," *Congressional Record,* Extensions of Remarks, vol. 115, part 6, May 21, 1969, 13380–81. To check on the status of the Equal Rights Amendment, go to equalrightsamendment.org. **92** Speech on more funding for public assistance: "Welfare Reform, A Beginning," *Congressional Record,* Extensions of Remarks, vol. 115, part 10, May 26, 1969, 13806. **93** Letter to Nixon: "A Letter to the President," *Congressional Record—House,* vol. 115, part 8, April 29, 1969, 10759. **94** Amnesty speech: "Amnesty for Men Resisting the War in Vietnam," *Congressional Record,* Extensions of Remarks, vol. 115, part 12, June 16, 1969, 15995–96.

Chapter 15: A Better Way

95 D.C. club reception: Ethel L. Payne, "So This Is Washington," *New Pittsburgh Courier,* January 11, 1969, 7. **95** Adelphi strike: "Rep. Chisholm Backs Hospital Strikers," *Amsterdam News,* February 1, 1969, 21. **95–96** "to its feet . . . dynamite": "Johnson Steps Down, Perry Up in Guardians," *Amsterdam News,* February 22, 1969, 4. **96** "shape up . . . leadership": "Schools Told to 'Shape Up,' " *South Bend Tribune,* March 20, 1969, 45. **97** "a new breed . . . promises": "Black Congresswoman Calls for Enforcing Rights Laws," *Atlanta Voice,* April 13, 1969, 2. **97** West Virginia highway workers: "Mrs. King Backs Fired Employe[e]s," *Courier-Journal* (Louisville, Kentucky), May 16, 1969, A16. **97** Parade: "Afro-American Day Marked in Harlem," *Kenosha News,* September 23, 1969, 2. **97** "we are fighting . . . wake up": Nanci, "Shirley Chisholm—She's Got 'People Power,' " *Democrat and Chronicle* (Rochester, New York), September 29, 1969, 8B. **97** "significant day . . .": "Moratorium Demonstrators Speak of Peace Peacefully," *Morning Call* (Allentown, Pennsylvania), October 16, 1969, 5. **97** "I talk to them about . . .": "Black Women in the Spotlight," *Florida Today,* November 23, 1969, 6D. **98** "The Urban Crisis": "Rep. Shirley Chisholm at St. Mary's on Tuesday," *Terre Haute Tribune-Star,* November 16, 1969, 30. **98** "The Social Revolution . . . Why Not?": "Rep. Shirley Chisholm to Give Talk at LCU," *La Crosse Tribune,* November 6, 1969, 11. **98** "While I do not . . . question": "Hope Is With Youth, Negro Diners Told," *Pittsburgh Press,* April 21, 1969, 2. **98** Speech at Howard: Shirley Chisholm, "Progress Through Understanding," *Congressional Record,* vol. 115, part 12, June 16, 1969, 15972–73. **98** On authenticity: Chisholm, *The Good Fight,* 13. **98–99** "for his deep understanding" and "closest advisers": Chisholm, *Unbought and Unbossed,* dedication page and 140. **99** Charlayne Hunter's review of *Unbought and Unbossed: New York Times Book Review,* November 1, 1970, 289–290. **99** Bills about Vietnam through gun control: *Congressional Record Index,* vol. 117, part 37, January 21, 1971, to December 17, 1971 (Washington, DC: U.S. Government Printing Office, 1971), 261–263. **100** "You wonder what is the use . . . the victors": Chisholm, *The Good Fight,* 14. **100** "promote the public welfare . . .": Wendy Maloney, "Trending: Congressional Black Caucus Takes Center Stage," *Library of Congress Blog,* September 20, 2017, https://blogs.loc.gov/loc/2017/09/trending-congressional-black-caucus-takes-center-stage/. **101** "Can a Woman Be a Good President?": Sara Slack and Tex Harris, "Can a Woman Be a Good President?," *Amsterdam News,* July 24, 1971, B1.

Chapter 16: Chizm for President

103 "I am black and I am a woman" and "Well, when are we going to break this tradition?": Chisholm, *The Good Fight,* 15. **103** First three headlines on Shirley running for president: "Shirley's Hat Tentatively in Big Ring," *Arizona Republic,* August 1, 1971, 12A; "For President: A Black Woman?," *Austin American-Statesman,* August 8, 1971, D18; and "Shirley's Sticking," *New York Daily News,* final edition, September 15, 1971, 8. **104** "A Rebel Bucks the System . . . reflective of America": Betsy Williams, "A Rebel Bucks the System," *Philadelphia Daily News,* December 30, 1971, 14. **104** "sparse" and "will have paved the way for change later on": Louis Salome, "Chisholm Campaign Is Off to a Slow Start," *Miami News,* January 5, 1972, 4A. **104** Tampa: Judy Hamilton, "Shirley Hopes Chisholm Is the One," *Tampa Times,* January 12, 1972, 7A. **105** Tallahassee: Chisholm, *The Good Fight,* 60–61. **105** "People, people, people . . . piercing": Sharon DeMarko, "I Am the People's Candidate and Must See to the People," *Pensacola Journal,* January 10, 1972, 1B. **105** "an important political announcement": Eugene Bogan, "3 Contenders Slate Stops in Pensacola," *Pensacola News,* January 17, 1972, 1. **106** "Chizm for President" incident: Chisholm, *The Good Fight,* 61.

Chapter 17: To Make That Someday Come
110 "I encouraged her . . . Fearless": Joy Miller, "Shirley Chisholm's Husband Contented Playing Second Fiddle to Strong-Willed Wife," *Oregonian*, February 23, 1972, 29. **110** "to make that someday come": Chisholm, *The Good Fight*, 3. **111** Position on criminal justice system: Chisholm, "Justice in America: Gun Control, Drug Abuse, Court, Police, Prison Reform, Political and Civil Dissent," *The Good Fight*, 174–184. **111** Position on the environment: "Our Environment," Presidential Campaign Position Paper no. 6, subgroup II, James Pitts, folder 26, Shirley Chisholm '72 Collection, Archives & Special Collections, Brooklyn College Library. **111** Position on health care: Chisholm, "The Cost of Care," *The Good Fight*, 193–199. **112** "The other candidates . . .": Chisholm, *The Good Fight*, 83. **112** "shaker-upper ...": Interview by Miriam Rosen, Pacifica Radio, June 1972, Chisholm, *Shirley Chisholm*, 37. **113** "seeing something . . .": Chisholm, *The Good Fight*, 87. **113** "I broke into tears . . . control of myself": Chisholm, *The Good Fight*, 87. **113** "Join with me on the Chisholm Trail! . . . governs our lives": Chisholm, *The Good Fight*, 88–89. **113–114** "A program . . . peak moment": Chisholm, *The Good Fight*, 89. **114** "We have all heard the tired . . . to lead": Chisholm, *The Good Fight*, 91. **114** "Sojourner . . . gets rough": Greg LeFever, "A Candidate on Pilgrimage," *Enquirer and News* (Battle Creek, Michigan), April 29, 1972, A1. **115** "If ever . . . but me?," "It was impossible for me . . . ," and "That unforgettable year . . . had to be taken": Chisholm, *The Good Fight*, 94, 95.

Chapter 18: Paving the Way
116 Secret Service detail: David Hess, "Candidates Risk Lives When They 'Press the Flesh'—Secret Service," *Charlotte Observer*, May 16, 1972, 2A. **116** "I don't care . . .": "Wallace Shooting Met With Horror, Dismay in Michigan," *Ironwood Daily Globe*, May 16, 1972, 6. **116** "Is that really you . . . and see you": Chisholm, *The Good Fight*, 97. She visited Wallace on June 8 ("Mrs. Chisholm Visits Wallace," *Ironwood Daily Globe*, June 8, 1972, 2). **116** "There were black politicians . . . cooked up!": Chisholm, *The Good Fight*, 97. **117** "that little black matriarch": Chisholm, *The Good Fight*, 32. **117** "the idea": Chisholm, *The Good Fight*, 74. **117** Smear campaign: Mackenzie Farkus, "As part of Watergate, FBI investigated a fake press release on Hubert Humphrey campaign stationery targeting Shirley Chisholm," muckrock.com, March 29, 2019, https://www.muckrock.com/news/archives/2019/mar/29/fbi-watergate-chisholm/. **117–118** "With tears streaming down my face . . .": John Lewis, Jr. "Chisholm Recalls Crying Over 'Dirty Tricks' Letter," *Baltimore Afro-American*, April 13, 1974, 1. **118** "Don't let the spirit die . . . moola": Lynch, *Chisholm '72—Unbought and Unbossed*, DVD. **119** Campaign funds spent and raised: Chisholm, *The Good Fight*, 45.

Chapter 19: Voice Was Needed
120 Bills in the 93rd Congress: Runaway Youth Act (HR 1751, HR 9942); Safe Schools Act (HR 2650); National Act for School Construction (HR 2892, HR 4068); Nutritional Labeling Act (HR 3702); Pure Foods Act (HR 3781); Handgun Control Act (HR 4267); National Healthcare Act (HR 5200); Prisoner Rights Act (HR 5202); Autistic Children Research Act (HR 5785); National Diabetes Act (HR 6193); Jeannette Rankin stamp (HR 9776). "Shirley Chisholm," congress.gov, https://www.congress.gov/member/shirley-chisholm/C000371?s=6&r=1&q=%7B%22search%22%3A%5B%22Shirley+Chisholm%22%5D%2C%22congress%22%3A93%7D. **120–121** Minimum wage bill, "Chisholm Provision," and "My own mother . . .": *Contact Shirley Chisholm: Your Voice in Congress*, Fall 1973, 4, http://www.avoiceonline.org/assets/njr-chisholm-5-5-1973fall/njr-chisholm-5-5-1973fall.pdf; and Martin Tolchin, "Mrs. Chisholm Led the Fight For Domestics' Base Pay," *New York Times*, June 21, 1973, 45. **121–122** "I have never worked so hard . . . Mrs. Chisholm's information!": Lesley Crosson, "Shirley Chisholm: Unbossed, Unbought and Undaunted," *Amsterdam News*, December 8, 1973, A5. **122** "Why is it that my private affairs . . .": Major Robinson, "My Marriage Is My Own Business—Chisholm," *Amsterdam News*, January 15, 1977, B1. **123** "They told me that my voice was needed . . . fight it out": John W. Lewis, Jr., "Fighter, Chisholm: 'I Get Adrenaline From the People,'" *Amsterdam News*, April 19, 1980, A4. **123** Battle for Office of Economic Opportunity: Lesley Crosson, "Shirley Chisholm: Unbossed, Unbought and Undaunted," *Amsterdam News*, December 8, 1973, A5. **123–124** School lunch program and WIC: "More Children Benefit From Lunch Program," *Amsterdam News*, May 14, 1975, B1. **124** "I have seen the results . . . educationally dead": John W. Lewis, Jr., "Fighter, Chisholm: 'I Get Adrenaline From the People,'" *Amsterdam News*, April 19, 1980. **124–128** Interview with Kathy Hacker: Kathy Hacker, "Chisholm Looks Back in Anger," *Philadelphia Inquirer*, December 13, 1982, 1C, 4C. **126–127** Cooper and Barrett article: "Chisholm's Compromise: Politics and the Art of Self-Interest," *Village Voice*, October 30, 1978, 1. **127** "The Democratic Party machine's . . . daggers were out at all times": Winslow, *Shirley Chisholm*, 146. **128** "You go and drown . . . I will make it": Jacqueline Trescott, "A Poignant Goodbye for Shirley Chisholm," *Courier-Journal* (Louisville, Kentucky), June 20, 1982, G5. **129** *Illusion of Inclusion*: "Putting It on Paper," *Philadelphia Inquirer*, January 31, 1993, A3.

Epilogue
130 "Mrs. Chisholm was . . .": James Barron, "Shirley Chisholm, 'Unbossed' Pioneer in Congress, Is Dead at 80," *New York Times*, January 3, 2005, https://www.nytimes.com/2005/01/03/obituaries/shirley-chisholm-unbossedpioneer-in-congress-is-dead-at-80.html. **130** "Throughout her life . . .": Harold Jackson, "Shirley Chisholm," *The Guardian*, January 3, 2005, https://www.theguardian.com/news/2005/jan/04/guardianobituaries.haroldjackson. **130** "She was a pioneer and a patriot . . .": T. Shawn Taylor, "Shirley Chisholm Admirers Share Fondest Memories," *Chicago Tribune*, January 12, 2005, section 8, 1. **130** "I don't think there's anyone . . .": Erin McClam, "Shirley Chisholm Recalled as Champion of Blacks, Women," *Morning Call*, January 4, 2005, A4. **130** "Perhaps if there was not a Shirley Chisholm . . .": "Mourners Recall a Committed Chisholm," *South Bend Tribune*, January 9, 2005, C10. **131** Women in the 109th Congress: "Women in the United States House of Representatives," Wikipedia, https://en.wikipedia.org/wiki/Women_in_the_United_States_House_of_Representatives. **131** Presidential Medal of Freedom ceremony, November 24, 2015, The White House, President Barack Obama, https://obamawhitehouse.archives.gov/the-press-office/2015/11/24/remarks-president-medal-freedom-ceremony. **131** "2019 Belongs to Shirley Chisholm": Jennifer Steinhauer, *New York Times*, July 6, 2019, https://www.nytimes.com/2019/07/06/sunday-review/

shirley-chisholm-monument-film.html. **132** "Shirley Chisholm fought . . .": "Governor Cuomo Announces Opening of $20 Million First Phase of Shirley Chisholm State Park in Brooklyn," July 2, 2019, https://www.governor.ny.gov/news/governor-cuomo-announces-opening-20-million-first-phase-shirley-chisholm-state-park-brooklyn. **132** "People want heroes . . .": Jennifer Steinhauer, "2019 Belongs to Shirley Chisholm," cited above. **132** "Shirley Chisholm created a path . . .": Melissa Wiley, *Insider,* January 20, 2021, https://www.insider.com/kamala-harris-purple-inauguration-outfit-inspiration-shirley-chisholm-2021-1. **132** "If they don't give you a seat at the table . . .": *People* staff, "1924-2005: Shirley Chisholm," *People,* January 17, 2005, https://people.com/archive/1924-2005-shirley-chisholm-vol-63-no-2/.

Author's Note
134 "Fighting Lady of Brooklyn": Leo J. Linder, "Boro Presents Biggest 3d Party Unit-Linder," *Brooklyn Eagle,* July 24, 1948, 2.

Back Cover
"If my story . . . ": Chisholm, *Unbought and Unbossed,* 187.

SELECTED SOURCES
ancestry.com. "New York, Passenger and Crew Lists (including Castle Garden and Ellis Island), 1820-1957"; "New York, New York, Marriage License Indexes, 1907-2018"; "New York, New York, Birth Index, 1910-1965"; and "U.S. WWII Draft Cards Young Men, 1940-1947"; and "U.S. Naturalization Records Indexes, 1794-1995."

Bureau of Community Statistical Services, Research Department. *Brooklyn Communities: Population Characteristics and Neighborhood Social Resources.* Volume 1. Community Council of Greater New York, 1959.

Chaudry, Ajay, et al. *Poverty in the United States: 50-Year Trends and Safety Net Impacts.* Office of Human Services Policy, Office of the Assistant Secretary for Planning and Evaluation, U.S. Department of Health and Human Services, March 2016.

Chisholm, Shirley. *The Good Fight.* Harper and Row, 1973.

_____. *Shirley Chisholm: The Last Interview and Other Conversations.* With an introduction by Barbara Lee. Melville House, 2021.

_____. *Unbought and Unbossed.* Expanded 40th Anniversary Edition with a foreword by Donna Brazile and an afterword by Shola Lynch. Take Root Media, 2010.

Cohen, Nancy L. "Why America Never Had Universal Child Care." *The New Republic,* April 24, 2013. https://newrepublic.com/article/113009/child-care-america-was-very-close-universal-day-care.

Colarossi, Natalie. "25 Vintage Photos Show How Desperate and Desolate America Looked During the Great Depression, the Last Time the Unemployment Rate Was as High as It Is Today." *Insider,* May 11, 2020. https://www.insider.com/great-depression-photos-of-america-unemployment-2020-5.

Dawkins, Wayne. *City Son: Andrew W. Cooper's Impact on Modern-Day Brooklyn.* University Press of Mississippi, 2012.

Dinkins, David, with Peter Knobler. *A Mayor's Life: Governing New York's Gorgeous Mosaic.* PublicAffairs, 2013.

English, David, and the staff of the *Daily Express. Divided They Stand: The American Election 1968.* Michael Joseph, 1969.

Fitzpatrick, Ellen. *The Highest Glass Ceiling: Women's Quest for the American Presidency.* Harvard University Press, 2016.

Gallagher, Julia A. *Black Women and Politics in New York City.* University of Illinois Press, 2012.

_____. "Waging 'The Good Fight': The Political Career of Shirley Chisholm, 1953-1982." *Journal of African American History,* Summer 2007, 392–416.

Gutgold, Nichola D. *Paving the Way for Madam President.* Lexington Books, 2006.

Hickling, Lee. "16 House Democrats Urge U.S. End War." *Evening Press* (Binghamton, New York), March 27, 1969, 10-C.

Howell, Ron. *Boss of Black Brooklyn: The Life and Times of Bertram L. Baker.* Empire State Editions, Fordham University Press, 2019.

Kazin, Alfred. *A Walker in the City.* Harvest, 1969.

Lynch, Shola, dir. *Chisholm '72—Unbought and Unbossed.* DVD. Twentieth Century Fox Home Entertainment, Inc., 2004.

Market, Howard. "Before Ebola, Ellis Island's Terrifying Medical Inspections." *PBS NewsHour,* October 15, 2014. https://www.pbs.org/newshour/health/october-15-1965-remembering-ellis-island.

Metcalf, George R. *Up From Within: Today's New Black Leaders.* Far-Eastern Book Co., 1973.

Miller, William H. "Italian Motor Ships: Saturnia & Vulcania." *PowerShips,* Summer 2018.

Purnell, Brian. *Fighting Jim Crow in the County of Kings: The Congress of Racial Equality in Brooklyn.* University Press of Kentucky, 2013.

Sokol, Jason. *All Eyes Are Upon Us: Race and Politics From Boston to Brooklyn.* Basic Books, 2014.

Spellen, Suzanne. "Walkabout: A Shirley Chisholm Architectural Walking Tour." Part 1. https://www.brownstoner.com/history/walkabout-a-shirley-chisholm-architectural-walking-tour-part-one/.

Wiberg, Eric. "SS Munamar, Munson Steamship Line, Carried Mail to Bahamas From US & Cuba in the 1920s." May 26, 2014. http://ericwiberg.com/2014/05/ss-munamar-munson-steamship-line-carried-mail-to-bahamas-from-us-cuba-in-the-1920s.

Wilder, Craig Steven. *A Covenant With Color: Race and Social Power in Brooklyn.* Columbia University Press, 2000.

Winslow, Barbara. *Shirley Chisholm: Catalyst for Change.* Routledge, 2013.

Woodsworth, Michael. *Battle for Bed-Stuy: The Long War on Poverty in New York City.* Harvard University Press, 2016.

★ ★ ★ ★ ★ ★ ★ ★ ★

ACKNOWLEDGMENTS

I am so grateful to my first editor, Priyanka Lamichhane, for her enthusiasm for the project. And I am equally grateful to my second and final editor, Angela Modany, for her terrific sensibilities, her probing mind, and for her all-around cheer and grace.

I'm indebted to others in the Nat Geo family who lent their brains and skills to the making of this book. Thank you, editorial director Becky Baines, executive editor Marfe Delano, fact-checker Robin Palmer, designer Julide Dengel, photo editor Sarah J. Mock, editorial production manager Joan Gossett, proofreader Gwenda Larsen, senior cartographer Mike McNey, and managing editor Vivian Suchman. Thank you to the team at Potomac Global Media: Kevin Mulroy, Barbara Brownell Grogan, Jane Sunderland, Kristin Sladen, and Christopher L. Mazzatenta.

There are people outside the Nat Geo family to thank for all sorts of help: Marianne LaBatto, associate archivist, and Colleen Bradley-Sanders, associate professor and college archivist, at Brooklyn College; Mary Jones and her colleagues at New York Public Library's Periodicals and Microforms Division, Stephen A. Schwarzman Building; Emily Carr, senior legal reference librarian, Global Legal Research Directorate, Law Library of Congress; Sheldon Lustig, VP/director of the New York Central System Historical Society; Desiree Alden-Gonzalez, collections manager, New York Transit Museum; Jennifer Govan with Library Service, Teachers College, Columbia University; Patricia Osbourne, transcript secretary, Office of the Registrar, Teachers College, Columbia University; and Shawn Purcell, senior librarian at the New York State Library's Cultural Education Center.

For insights on Shirley Chisholm and Brooklyn and for reading the manuscript, thank you Wayne Dawkins, associate professor at Morgan State University and author of *City Son: Andrew W. Cooper's Impact on Modern-Day Brooklyn*. For also reading the manuscript and providing valuable information, thank you Zinga A. Fraser, PhD, assistant professor in Brooklyn College's African Studies Department and Women's and Gender Studies Program. And thank you, Melvin McCray III, journalist and filmmaker, for information on Chisholm and Brooklyn. For help with all things Bajan, thank you, Karen Best.

I'm also grateful to my sister, Nelta, for her feedback on the manuscript and to my agent, Jennifer Lyons, for all the many things she does in support of me and my work.

INDEX